Editor-in-Chief and Founder:
  Lyndon H. LaRouche, Jr.
Editorial Board: *Lyndon H. LaRouche, Jr. , Helga
  Zepp-LaRouche, Robert Ingraham, Tony
  Papert, Gerald Rose, Dennis Small, Jeffrey
  Steinberg, William Wertz*
Co-Editors: *Robert Ingraham, Tony Papert*
Technology: *Marsha Freeman*
Transcriptions: *Katherine Notley*
Ebooks: *Richard Burden*
Graphics: *Alan Yue*
Photos: *Stuart Lewis*
Circulation Manager: *Stanley Ezrol*

INTELLIGENCE DIRECTORS
Economics: *Marcia Merry Baker, Paul Gallagher*
History: *Anton Chaitkin*
Ibero-America: *Dennis Small*
Russia and Eastern Europe: *Rachel Douglas*
United States: *Debra Freeman*

INTERNATIONAL BUREAUS
Bogotá: *Miriam Redondo*
Berlin: *Rainer Apel*
Copenhagen: *Tom Gillesberg*
Lima: *Sara Madueño*
Melbourne: *Robert Barwick*
Mexico City: *Gerardo Castilleja Chávez*
New Delhi: *Ramtanu Maitra*
Paris: *Christine Bierre*
Stockholm: *Ulf Sandmark*
United Nations, N.Y.C.: *Leni Rubinstein*
Washington, D.C.: *William Jones*
Wiesbaden: *Göran Haglund*

ON THE WEB
e-mail: eirns@larouchepub.com
www.larouchepub.com
www.executiveintelligencereview.com
www.larouchepub.com/eiw
Webmaster: *John Sigerson*
Assistant Webmaster: *George Hollis*
Editor, Arabic-language edition: *Hussein Askary*

EIR (ISSN 0273-6314) *is published weekly
(50 issues), by EIR News Service, Inc.,
P.O. Box 17390, Washington, D.C. 20041-0390.
(703) 297-8434*

European Headquarters: E.I.R. GmbH, Postfach
Bahnstrasse 9a, D-65205, Wiesbaden, Germany
Tel: 49-611-73650
Homepage: http://www.eir.de
e-mail: info@eir.de
Director: Georg Neudecker

Montreal, Canada: 514-461-1557
eir@eircanada.ca

Denmark: EIR - Danmark, Sankt Knuds Vej 11,
basement left, DK-1903 Frederiksberg, Denmark.
Tel.: +45 35 43 60 40, Fax: +45 35 43 87 57. e-mail:
eirdk@hotmail.com.

Mexico City: EIR, Sor Juana Inés de la Cruz 242-2
Col. Agricultura C.P. 11360
Delegación M. Hidalgo, México D.F.
Tel. (5525) 5318-2301
eirmexico@gmail.com

Copyright: ©2018 EIR News Service. All rights
reserved. Reproduction in whole or in part without
permission strictly prohibited.

Canada Post Publication Sales Agreement
#40683579

Postmaster: Send all address changes to *EIR*, P.O.
Box 17390, Washington, D.C. 20041-0390.

Signed articles in *EIR* represent the views of the authors,
and not necessarily those of the Editorial Board.

As Election Day Approaches, the British Have Overplayed Their Hand

As Election Day Approaches, the British Have Overplayed their Hand

Oct. 17—In the final countdown to the 2018 midterm elections, an important question on the minds of potential voters is exactly what really happened in 2016. Yes, a foreign power intervened massively to fix the election result beforehand. At the same time, that power created a backup plan to ensure that if Donald Trump were elected despite its efforts, it would be able to paralyze and destroy his incoming Administration and remove him from office.

This foreign power was not Putin's Russia, but the British Empire. As *EIR* has documented in depth for the past two years, the phony evidentiary basis for the charges of Russian intervention and of Trump's "collusion" with Russia, originally consisted of nothing but false evidence planted on Trump associates by British agents on British soil. The tactical leader of the British plot was Sir Richard Dearlove, the former head of the British Secret Intelligence Service (MI6) who also led the fabrication of the "dirty dossier" on purported Iraqi weapons of mass destruction for the catastrophic Iraq War of 2003 to date. Christopher Steele fabricated his own "dossier" under the same Dearlove. British intelligence figures Alexander Downer, Stefan Halper, Joseph Mifsud and many others developed the entrapment of Trump-linked figures on British soil, sometimes summoning them to London for that purpose. Even the handover of Steele's dossier to the late Sen. John McCain's office occurred in Britain's former Dominion of Canada, not in the United States.

On Oct. 15, the nationally prominent lawyer Joseph diGenova, a former U.S. Attorney for Washington, D.C., gave an explosive interview to WMAL radio there.

The following is a paraphrase of some of his remarks.

DiGenova: This is why the British are scared.... British MI6 conducted illegal electronic surveillance on U.S. citizens at the request of the FBI and [CIA's] Brennan. That's how they found out [George] Papadopoulos was not interested in Hillary's emails or anything else. Illegal spying by the Brits. That's why the Brits are going crazy.

That's a remarkable issue. We talk about domestic surveillance all the time. But when you stretch out to work with foreign governments—read "collude"—to spy on an American citizen, that really opens up an entirely different can of worms.

It opens up a huge criminal liability on the part of American intelligence officials, especially Brennan. Brennan actually visited London, before all this started, and visited MI6 and GCHQ before it started....

WMAL: The President has chosen not to declassify certain documents....

DiGenova: Trump won't declassify certain

documents because two foreign governments asked him not to.

This is a different President. He is now in full control of his Presidency. He is playing everyone in his orbit. He knows exactly what needs to be made public, and is holding it close to his vest. He is playing it like a masterful Stradivarius—for when it will have maximum impact; to use it at the maximum moment. Trump is in full control of his Presidency. You saw it last night with Lesley Stahl, when he said, "I'm President, and you're not." Throwing it in her face....

Obama's illegal spying will have two political consequences. Trump understands the coup against him.... He is not trying to measure the election; he understands that the coup was so massive; why Susan Rice did her famous email to herself on inauguration day. Why you see stories of her [saying], of course the White House knew about the Russiagate thing. They were involved in it, so that if Trump refused to accept election results, they'd have a way to undercut his legitimacy.

WMAL: Will we see this information ahead of election day?

DiGenova: I don't know. Trump is in full control. He knows Mueller's investigation is over because it was illegal. Because of British spying, which our FBI asked them to do. So much worse than Watergate! If Republicans lose the House, these investigations are over, because [Senate Intelligence Chair] Burr is a chicken—the only way it will come out is through a criminal investigation by DOJ, and that won't happen unless Sessions and Rosenstein are gone after the election.

If we lose the House, all of the investigations come to an end. Every one of them. Because the people in the Senate have no "*cojones.*"

WMAL: I hope Trump declassifies the FISA warrants. What's in them?

DiGenova: They will show Halper used a CIA agent to entrap Papadopoulos and [Carter] Page, and funnel back to the U.S., to the FBI, to get the FISA warrant. [To get British intelligence agencies] MI6 and GCHQ to do illegal overseas surveillance of the these people—totally illegal! The application [for a FISA warrant] presents [Page] as in cahoots. They knew it was all fabricated.

In his interview, diGenova spoke as though the British intervention was triggered by requests from Obamatons James Comey and others, and it may well look that way when based only on currently available information and the delimiting factor of a purely U.S. domestic viewpoint. But that does not take into account Barack Obama's longstanding service to British imperial goals, or the fact that the British viewed Donald Trump and those around him as mortal threats dating as far back as 2014. It does not take into account the longstanding service of American intelligence agencies to British imperial goals, particularly when it comes to waging asymmetrical war against Russia and China. That is the true meaning of the so-called "special relationship"—free use of American brawn to pursue British imperial goals. That is also why complete declassification of all British-originated documents associated with the coup, dating from Stefan Halper's operations against Michael Flynn back in 2014, must be subject to full declassification by the President. Nothing less than the future existence of the United States is at stake.

EIR Contents

www.larouchepub.com Volume 45, Number 42, October 19, 2018

Cover This Week

Washington before Yorktown (1781), painted 1824-1825 by Rembrandt Peale (1778-1860).

AS ELECTION DAY APPROACHES, THE BRITISH HAVE OVERPLAYED THEIR HAND

2 EDITORIAL
As Election Day Approaches, the British Have Overplayed Their Hand

I. The Fight on the Economy

5 Public Credit: Cutting the Gordian Knot with the Sword of Damocles
by William Wertz

15 National Sovereignty and a New Bretton Woods
by Robert Ingraham

21 South Dakota Congressional Candidate Wieczorek Hosts Tri-State Meeting, Backing a New 'Just' World System
by Marcia Merry Baker and Jason Ross

II. A Moment of Decision

25 ZEPP-LAROUCHE WEBCAST
The Stakes in the U.S. Midterm Elections: War or Peace

33 Mike Pence's Dumb Ass Speech on China: When the Cat's Away, the Mice Will Play
by Barbara Boyd

III. Non-Linear Economics

40 Riemann Refutes Euler: Behind an Earthshaking Scientific Discovery
by Lyndon H. LaRouche, Jr.
November 3, 1995

I. The Fight on the Economy

Public Credit: Cutting the Gordian Knot with the Sword of Damocles

by William Wertz

The following is an edited transcript of a presentation given by Will Wertz to the LaRouche PAC Manhattan meeting, on Saturday, October 13, 2018.

I named this presentation "Cutting the Gordian Knot with the Sword of Damocles." For those who are not familiar with those two terms, let me just say that the Sword of Damocles has come to represent a looming danger. For instance, in 1961 President John F Kennedy referred to the nuclear Sword of Damocles hanging over humanity. Today, you might look at the situation from the standpoint of the threat of nuclear war if the British Empire were successful in carrying out a coup against the President of the United States and in continuing to pursue its geopolitical policy in opposition to Russia in particular. We also are faced with a Damocles' Sword in respect to the potential for a financial blow-out of the entire trans-Atlantic system, should the necessary solutions not be implemented.

Now the problem here is the Gordian Knot. We are faced with a certain impasse. The Gordian Knot was a knot that people were challenged to untie, and Alexander the Great solved the problem. He took out a sword and cut the knot. In a very real sense, that's what we must do today. Another way of putting it is, as Lyndon LaRouche has often stated, necessity will be the mother of invention.

We are in a situation where we have a President of the United States who is unique. He is committed to reversing certain policies which Lyndon LaRouche has opposed for decades. The policy of free trade; the policy of a post-industrial society; the policy of globalization; out-sourcing of jobs from this country and other advanced sector countries. He has opposed the Paris Climate Treaty, recognizing that this is illegitimate and if implemented would result in the destruction of human life and human productive activity. During the campaign, Trump said that he was in favor of Glass-Steagall, the law that was implemented in the 1930s under Franklin Roosevelt that separated commercial banking

C-SPAN

President Trump speaking at a campaign rally in Southaven, Mississippi on Oct. 2, 2018.

oriented toward productive investment, from speculative Wall Street investments. He also, by the way, referred to the fact that there is a financial bubble. Then in March of 2017, he made a remarkable series of speeches in Michigan, Kentucky, and Washington, D.C., in which he advocated explicitly the American System— or what he called the American model.

A True Revolution in the Making

What I would like to do is to reference excerpts from those three speeches, both to give you a sense of the potential for implementing the American System under President Trump, should we be successful, as we must, in defeating the British coup attempt against him. But also, to indicate an area of omission which must be corrected in his understanding of the American system.

So, let me begin with his speech of March 15, 2017 in Willow Run, Michigan. At that time, he said:

> Our great Presidents, from Washington to Jefferson to Jackson to Lincoln, all understood that a great nation must protect its manufacturing, must protect itself from the outside.... We must embrace a new economic model. Let's call it 'The American Model.' Under this system, we will reduce burdens on our companies and on our businesses. But, in exchange, companies must hire and grow in America. They must hire and grow in our country. That is how we will succeed and grow together—American workers and American industry side-by-side. Nobody can beat us. Because whether we are rich or poor, young or old, black or brown or white, we all bleed the same red blood of patriots.... Great Americans of all backgrounds built the Arsenal of Democracy—including the legendary Rosie the Riveter, who worked here at Willow Run.... Now, these hundreds of acres that defended our democracy are going to help build the cars and cities of the future ... so I ask you today to join me in daring to believe that this facility, this city, and this nation will once again shine with industrial might....

Poster by J. Howard Miller

Rosie the Riveter.

I'm asking all of the companies here today to join us in this new Industrial Revolution.

Five days later, President Trump spoke at Freedom Hall in Louisville, Kentucky. An excerpt from his speech follows:

> Our first Republican President, Abraham Lincoln, was born right here in Kentucky.... And the great 19th Century American statesman, Henry Clay, represented Kentucky in the United States Congress. Henry Clay believed in what he called the American System, and proposed tariffs to protect American industry, and finance American infrastructure.... Clay was a fierce advocate for American manufacturing.... He said, very strongly: Free trade, which would throw wide open our ports to foreign production without duties, while theirs remains closed to us.... Clay said that trade must be fair, equal, and reciprocal.... For too long, our government has abandoned the American System.

> Finally, the next day—March 21—President Trump addressed the National Republican Congressional Committee dinner in Washington, D.C.:

> I have called this model ... the American Model. And this is the system that our Founders wanted. Our greatest American leaders—including George Washington, Hamilton, Jackson, Lincoln—they all agreed that for America to be a strong nation it must also be a great manufacturing nation.... The Republican platform of 1896—more than a century ago— stated that: "Protection and reciprocity are twin measures of American policy and go hand in hand.".... The platform went on to say: "We renew and emphasize our allegiance to the policy of protection, as the bulwark of American industrial independence and the foundation of American development and prosperity..."

Our first Republican President, Abraham Lincoln, ran his first campaign for public office

National Park Service

President Dwight Eisenhower signing H.R. 8127, the Highway Bill, on May 6, 1954.

in 1832, when he was only 23 years old. He began by imagining the benefits a railroad could bring to his part of Illinois, without ever having seen a steam-powered train. He had no idea, and yet he knew what it could be. Thirty years later, as President, Lincoln signed the law that built the first Transcontinental Railroad, uniting our country from ocean to ocean. . . .

Another great Republican President, Dwight Eisenhower, had a vision of a national infrastructure plan. As an officer in the Army after World War I, he joined a military convoy that trekked across the nation to the Pacific Coast. It traveled along the Lincoln Highway—called then the Lincoln Highway. Its journey began by the South Lawn of the White House, at a monument known today as Zero Milestone. . . . The journey made a great impression on the then-young Eisenhower. More than three decades later, as President, he signed the bill that created our great Interstate Highway System—once again uniting us as a nation. Now is time for a new Republican administration, working with our Republican Congress, to pass the next great infrastructure bill.

So, I think that gives you a sense of the thinking of President Trump, who even in his recent speeches at rallies over the last few days, has been emphasizing the importance of increasing blue-collar employment in this country, reversing the de-industrialization which has occurred. It must be noted that since September 2017, 2.5 million jobs have been created in this country; 640,000 of those in goods producing, including manufacturing, construction, mining, and transport; 260,000 of those in manufacturing over the last year. So, some progress has been made. However, the purpose of this presentation today is to emphasize a big omission thus far in terms of what he has presented as the means for implementing and financing his goals.

This has real implications in terms of the upcoming discussion of a major infrastructure policy in this country. It also has major implications in terms of the necessary Four Power agreement among the United States, Russia, China, and India—among other potential countries such as Japan and South Korea—to build a New Bretton Woods System that will make possible the development of the entire planet; the exploration of space; the development of new forms of energy such as fusion power; and the expansion of capital goods production in this country, as well as other countries for that purpose—resulting in the creation of millions of productive jobs. In a certain sense, the two areas that we must concentrate on are infrastructure development in the United States; and on the other hand, the export of capital goods to develop the rest of the planet, even as we unite to develop mankind's mastery over space.

Constitutional Credit Issuance

Now, the area of omission that I want to address is the area of financing of these developments that are required for humanity. Part of LaRouche PAC's platform to secure the future of America is Lyndon LaRouche's Four Laws. That includes the implementation of Glass-Steagall, which is yet to be done. It includes an emphasis on productive investment to increase the productive powers of labor through an emphasis on capital-intensive forms of production. It includes space exploration and the development of fusion power. Those are the first, third, and fourth of LaRouche's Four Laws. The second law is, in a certain sense, the crucial element here.

I'll read that second law:

A return to a system of top-down and thoroughly defined national banking. The tested successful model to be authorized is that which had been instituted under the direction of the policies of national banking which had been actually successfully installed under President Abraham

The British Have Overplayed Their Hand

An 1861 $10 Demand Note (Greenback).

Lincoln's superseding authority of a currency created by the Presidency of the United States; that is, the greenbacks. As conducted as a national banking and credit system placed under the supervision of the Office of the Treasury Secretary of the United States.

The problem is that if you look at the Presidents of the United States who President Trump referred to—Washington, Jefferson, Andrew Jackson, Abraham Lincoln—only two of those were for national banking and national banking credit to facilitate manufacturing development—that is, George Washington, whose Secretary of the Treasury was the author of the First National Bank of the United States, and who defended the constitutionality of that National Bank, and Abraham Lincoln, the first Republican President, who advocated "greenbacks" as legal tender. These were currency notes, Treasury notes, issued to fund the Civil War, which also facilitated the economic development of the United States following the Civil War. He also advocated a National Currency and Banking Act, which passed in 1863-64 following the greenback policy which was passed in February of 1862.

The two others, Jefferson and Jackson, were thoroughly opposed to these policies. Jefferson wrote an opinion, as did the Attorney General of the United States at the time, opposing Hamilton, saying that because the Constitution did not explicitly call for a National Bank, it was unconstitutional. Andrew Jackson, when he was re-elected in 1832, vetoed the Second National Bank.

So, you have a certain contradiction here, and it needs to be resolved if we are to have the American System of political economy, as it was developed by Alexander Hamilton and continued by Abraham Lincoln, as well as later by such Presidents as McKinley (whom President Trump has also referred to), and Franklin Roosevelt, whose Arsenal for Democracy President Trump referenced in his speech in Detroit, and whose Glass-Steagall bill President Trump supported, at least during the campaign. We must recognize that LaRouche's second law is absolutely necessary. We need the equivalent today of Lincoln's greenback policy.

Crucial Role of the Greenback Policy

I'm going to present a short history of the fight for the greenback under Lincoln. You will see that the fight for the greenback was very much part of this fight for national banking. Going back to even before the United States of America was created, going back to the 1600s in the Massachusetts Bay Colony, it was a fundamental issue. I would even say that the American Revolution was not so much about taxation without representation (although it was definitely a factor). More fundamentally, it was about the British Empire's opposition to the initial colonies, and then the United States of America exercising its sovereign right to create bills of credit to facilitate the development of the productive powers of its population.

My associate at *Executive Intelligence Review*, Paul Gallagher, recommended a book which is very instructive. It's called *The History of the Legal Tender Paper Money Issued During the Great Rebellion, Being a Loan Without Interest and a National Currency.*

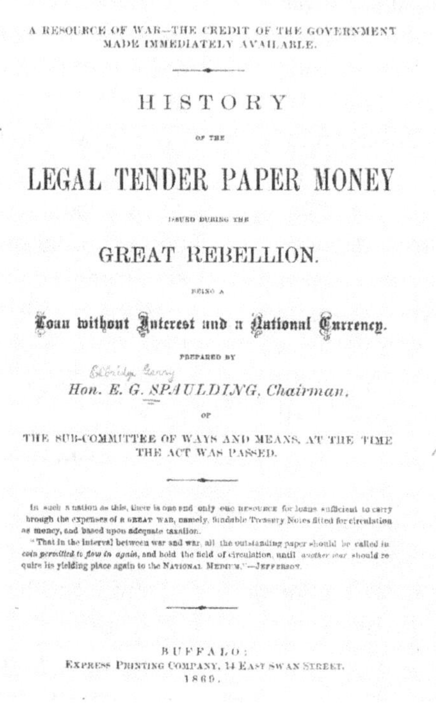

A RESOURCE OF WAR—THE CREDIT OF THE GOVERNMENT MADE IMMEDIATELY AVAILABLE.

HISTORY

OF THE

LEGAL TENDER PAPER MONEY

ISSUED DURING THE

GREAT REBELLION.

BEING A

Loan without Interest and a National Currency.

PREPARED BY

Hon. E. G. SPAULDING, Chairman,

OF

THE SUB-COMMITTEE OF WAYS AND MEANS, AT THE TIME THE ACT WAS PASSED.

BUFFALO:
EXPRESS PRINTING COMPANY, 14 EAST SWAN STREET.
1869.

This book was prepared by the Hon. Elbridge Gerry Spaulding, who was chairman of the Sub-committee of Ways and Means at the time the greenback policy was passed in 1862. The book, published in 1869, contains the actual history of the debates around the greenback policy, and around the National Currency and Banking Act of 1863-64.

So, who was Elbridge Gerry Spaulding? He originally ran for Congress as a Whig candidate and served one term. He became the New York Treasurer in 1854-55, and then ran for Congress again, this time as a Republican, and served two terms in Congress. In 1860, he made a very famous speech denouncing slavery and calling upon the Republican Party to back Abraham Lincoln. I found this book to be quite extraordinary. The first thing you have to understand is that the government did not have money to pay the soldiers; we were faced with a rebellion, a secession backed by foreign countries—i.e., the British—and we did not have the funds to pay the Army or the Navy. The bankers on Wall Street wanted to profit from the war (some things apparently haven't changed all that much)—they were holding out to be able to be the brokers, the money changers for the government. On Saturday, January 11, 1862, a delegation of these bankers descended upon Washington, D.C. What Spaulding wrote is as follows:

> Delegates from some of the banks in New York, Boston and Philadelphia, appeared in Washington to oppose the bill.... Mr. James Gallatin, of New York, (National Bank) made the principal speech against legal tender.

Spaulding objected to any and every form of what was referred to as "shinning" by government through Wall Street or State Street. He finished his comments by firmly refusing to assent to any scheme which would permit speculation by brokers, bankers and others in government securities. The book then refers to many letters that he received backing him up in this. One letter he received said, "I trust both Houses will put it right along through, regardless of what the New York

Hon. Elbridge Gerry Spaulding, c. 1860-65.

note-shavers and usurers may say." So, this was the real issue here. The question of whether or not the rebellion could be crushed depended on defeating the Wall Street, the State Street, and the Chestnut Street bankers (from New York, Boston, and Philadelphia). And in asserting the sovereign powers of the United States not to be subservient to these private banking interests, who in some cases were allied with Britain.

The fundamental Constitutional issue involved at this point was cited explicitly by Spaulding; that is, Article I, Clause 18 of the Constitution, which reads: "To make all Laws which shall be necessary and proper for carrying into Execution the foregoing Powers, and all other Powers vested by this Constitution in the Government of the United States, or in any Department or Officer thereof."

This is the section of the Constitution which Alexander Hamilton specifically cited in his defense of the constitutionality of the National Bank. It's referred to as the Implied Powers. Under the Articles of Confederation, all you had were express powers; there was an enumeration of the powers that could be exerted. But in the U.S. Constitution, there are not only express powers, but there are implied powers. This particular section of the Constitution is referred to as the Elastic Clause, because it allows for the government to exercise its sovereignty and determine what measures are necessary and proper to carry out the powers which are invested in the government by We, the People, particularly as expressed in the *Preamble* to the Constitution—that is, the necessity of Promoting the General Welfare and Providing for the Common Defense in particular.

Spaulding is very explicit in his remarks that this is particularly the case with the National Currency and Banking Act. He says, "I have no doubt that the general principle of the National Banking bill proposed by the Secretary of the Treasury is Constitutional." He says explicitly, "See Hamilton's celebrated argument presented to President Washington in favor of the constitutionality of the United States Bank in 1791."

I will also say that in this book and in this discussion, it's a very rich discussion. It was well understood by the Congressmen—and particularly by Spaulding—what the position was of Jefferson and Andrew Jackson. What Spaulding says in one of his speeches is as follows:

> It is now most apparent that the policy advocated by Alexander Hamilton of a strong central government was the true policy. Jefferson opposed the creation of all banks, both state and national. Alexander Hamilton proposed a National Bank during the struggle for American independence in 1780, but his suggestions were not then adopted. During Washington's administration in 1791, the First Bank of the United States was incorporated, mainly under the influence of Mr. Hamilton, which continued in operation until 1811 when its charter expired. No national bank was in existence during the second war with Great Britain [that is, the War of 1812—wfw]. In 1816, the Second Bank of the United States was chartered and continued its existence until 1836, when its charter again expired. All will remember the decided opposition of General Jackson to its recharter, and the fierce struggle that ensued between the friends and opponents of the United States Bank. Friends of the Bank were finally beaten when Jackson was re-elected President in the Fall of 1832. The friends of the United States Bank again rallied in 1840-41 but were again defeated by the veto of John Tyler.

So, you see, this was an ongoing struggle, and *Jefferson and Andrew Jackson were on the wrong side. I think we need to bring this to the attention of President Trump; he may not be aware of that.* This issue is very important, because the policies of Hamilton and Lincoln are the policies which are required today, as expressed in Lyndon LaRouche's second law.

Sculpture by James Earl Fraser

Statue of Alexander Hamilton in front of the Treasury Building, Washington, DC.

America: Built Through Public Credit

I'll continue with further quotes from Spaulding:

> In carrying on the existing war, and putting down the rebellion, it is necessary to bring into exercise all the sovereign power of the Government to sustain itself.... This bill is a necessary means of carrying into execution the powers granted in the Constitution "to raise and support armies," and "to provide and maintain a navy"...

Alexander Hamilton, in discussing these high powers of the Constitution says: "These powers ought to exist, *without limitation*; because it is impossible to foresee or define the extent and variety of national exigencies and the correspondent extent and variety of the means necessary to satisfy them...."

It must be admitted as a necessary consequence, that there can be *no limitation* of that authority which is to provide for the defense and protection of the community in any matter essential to its efficacy; that is, in any matter essential to the formation, direction, or support of the *NATIONAL FORCES*. (This idea is from *The Federalist Papers*). "I am unwilling that this Government, with all its immense power and resources, should be left in the hands of any class of men, bankers or money-lenders....

Why, then, should it go into Wall street, State street, Chestnut street, or any other street begging for money?...

The powers of the Government were given for the welfare of the nation.... We need it to prevent foreign intervention.

Congressman Kellogg from Illinois spoke and said the following:

The powers of the Old World, who have looked

with a jealous eye on the mighty progress of the Western Continent, are seeking occasion to cripple our onward and upward career.... Our Government antagonizes theirs. The principles are different.... We must take all the power we have, we must throw every energy, all the means of our Government in the direction of the war power, for the purpose of self-preservation and perpetuation.

Senator Wilson of Massachusetts commented: "It is a contest between brokers, and jobbers, and money-changers on the one side,"—(think of Franklin Roosevelt's inaugural speech where he talked about the money changers in Wall Street)—"and the people of the United States on the other. I venture to express the opinion that ninety-nine of every hundred of the loyal people of the United States are for this legal tender clause."

Then Senator Sumner of Massachusetts gave something of a history of the fight for bills of credit, beginning before the year 1700. Spaulding quotes from Sumner:

It appears that the phrase "bills of credit," was familiarly used for bank notes as early as 1683, in England, and also as early as 1714 in New England. But the first issue in America was in 1690, by the Colony of Massachusetts, and the occasion, identical with the present, was to pay soldiers returning unexpectedly from an unsuccessful expedition against Canada.

Mr. Sumner went into a brief history of the issue of bills of credit—paper money— in the States of Massachusetts, Rhode Island, Connecticut, Virginia and North Carolina, which led to the passage of an act by the Imperial Parliament,... in 1751, which expressly forbade the issue of

Julian Vannerson

Rep. William Kellogg, Dec. 31, 1858.

Mathew Brady

Sen. Charles Sumner (1811-1874).

any paper bills, or bills of credit, except for certain specific purposes, or upon certain specified emergencies; and declaring that such paper money should not be a legal tender for private debts. Continental paper money was issued during the Revolutionary War, not made a legal tender by Congress, although the States were recommended to make them such. He argued at great length the power of Congress to issue Treasury notes and make them a legal tender; and that it was purposely left by the framers of the Constitution to the sound discretion of Congress, in great emergencies, to decide whether it was necessary to exercise the power or not.

What he is referring to is that in 1686, there was an attempt to create a bank of credit in the Massachusetts Colony. There was a document published in 1687 which spelled out what the plan was:

By [the Bank], the trade and wealth of this country [will be] established upon its own foundation and upon a medium or balance arising within itself, viz., the lands and products of this country; and not upon the importation of gold or silver or the scarcity or plenty of them, or of anything else from foreign nations, which may be withheld, prohibited or enhanced, at their pleasure.

This was suppressed—this entire operation in the colonies to issue their own bills of credit to create a bank of credit to essentially finance the development of the early colonies.

In 1781, before there was a new Constitution, Alexander Hamilton wrote, "The tendency of a National Bank is to increase public and private credit. Industry is increased, commodities are multiplied, agriculture and manufactures flourish, and herein consists the true wealth and prosperity of the state." In 1795, in one of his four Reports to the U.S. Congress on Public Credit, he wrote:

Public Credit … is among the principal engines of useful enterprise and internal improvement.… It is by credit that he is enabled to procure the tools, the materials, and even the subsistence of which he stands in need, until his industry has supplied him with capital; and, even then, he derives, from an established and increased credit, the means of extending his undertakings.

only for the repair of existing infrastructure. It does not include investments needed to build up the infrastructure of the country.

Look at these two figures: $14 trillion made available to the financial sector by agencies of our federal government, with none of it going to productive investment; and $5 trillion as a low estimate of what's required to just repair our existing infrastructure, not even to build new infrastructure. That makes very clear that the only way to fund the required infrastructure is by returning to these national banking credit policies of Hamilton and Abraham Lincoln, and rejecting the arguments of Thomas Jefferson and Andrew Jackson. This is what is required.

The Failed Federal Reserve

I think it should be clear from this documentation that the fight for the greenbacks, is a fight which continues to this day. After the greenbacks were ended with the Specie Resumption Act in 1875, the U.S. government lost its ability to extend sovereign credit, as was done with the greenbacks. Instead what we got in 1913 was the Federal Reserve system, which does not extend credit for productive purposes.

Here are some useful statistics about the Federal Reserve, and what our infrastructure deficit is in this country. Sheila Bair, in testimony to the House Financial Services Committee in 2012, said that the Federal Reserve, the Federal Deposit Insurance Corporation (FDIC), and the Treasury made just over $14 trillion available to the financial sector. The Fed itself made approximately $9 trillion available, which began in 2007, before the 2008 collapse. *None* of that went to productive investment. It went to bailing out banks which had brought the crisis on themselves, by their lobbying for the repeal of Glass-Steagall, and through their opposition to the kind of credit policy which Lyndon LaRouche has advocated and continues to advocate today.

Now, the American Society of Civil Engineers has estimated that the total infrastructure deficit in the United States is at least $5 trillion, but that $5 trillion is

LaRouche on Credit

It is precisely this element, the second law that Lyndon LaRouche put forward, which is currently missing, and which must—*must*—be implemented, if we're to get out of the crisis that we're in right now.

Lyndon LaRouche has addressed this repeatedly over the decades. And he has specifically called for the U.S. Treasury to take over the Federal Reserve Bank and the Federal Reserve System, and to issue fiat credit, which would then be conducted through the banking system to productive investment in the United States, and also the same mechanism can be used to fund exports, which is of particular importance in terms of the question of credit extension as part of a New Bretton Woods system.

In 1980, LaRouche wrote a pamphlet entitled, "Why Credit Can Be Greatly Expanded Without Adding to Inflation." I'll read a quote from that, because I think it makes very clear how this can be done today, essentially following on the policies of the greenback under Lincoln.

In the section entitled "The Creation of Credit," LaRouche proposed to generate—

…fiat credit in the form of currency notes issued through national banking.… The new notes are not to be issued against federal government operating deficits, but on capital account. The new currency notes are to be put into circulation through national banking channels, such as participation in loans issued for hard-commodity production and productive capital loans through the local private bankers of ultimate borrowers.

Therefore, the amount of fiat credit put into circulation through such channels is regulated by the following principal considerations. It is limited by loan demand on account of tangible production's capacity, technological improvement, and operating capital requirements, and by the demand for such uses of credit among creditworthy borrowers. Each increment of new fiat credit issued through such channels supplements private banking capital also participating in the loan. Therefore, fiat credit is not put into circulation except against a matching increase in newly produced, tangible wealth providing security for this credit issuance....

Governmental fiat credit should be issued, except under conditions of national emergencies such as wars, only in the form of currency notes loaned on capital account, either to economic ventures of governments (wealth-creating state investments), or through private banks as partici-

---

Draft Federal Reserve Nationalization Act

These are excerpts from Lyndon LaRouche's "Draft Federal Reserve Nationalization Act of 1992," presented as Appendix B in The LaRouche Program to Save The Nation, *published by LaRouche's Committee for a New Bretton Woods in May 1998 (153-page paperback).*

Productive Credit via Discount Window

The Act proposes that new long-term, low-interest credit in the amount of approximately $1 trillion per annum be issued by the U.S. Treasury via the new National Bank to the U.S. physical economy by an entirely new mechanism. The National Bank is to open wide its discount window for general lending of directed credit to the productive, infrastructure, and related sectors of the physical economy ...

All new credit and currency of the U.S.A. is to be thus issued by the U.S. Treasury under Article 1 of the Constitution, as U.S. Treasury bills ...

Of the total $1 trillion per annum issued, approximately $600 billion is to be spent by the U.S. Treasury itself in the form of basic economic infrastructure projects, run by federal, state, and local agencies and subsidiaries ...

These government projects will generate additional credit demand in the area of another $400 billion per annum of purchases and investments by private-sector firms to be engaged in supplying these government projects, for a total of $1 trillion new productive activity.

The New 'National Bank of the United States'

Section 1. Section 1 of the Federal Reserve Act of 1913 is hereby amended to read: "Under Article 1 of the Constitution pertaining to the monopoly of the U.S. government in emitting legal tender, the Federal Reserve System is hereby nationalized and placed under the jurisdiction of the Department of the Treasury of the United States. Its name is hereby changed to the National Bank of the United States."

Section 2. Section 1 of the Federal Reserve Act is hereby amended to read: "The Federal Reserve shall immediately cease issuance of Federal Reserve notes as legal tender. As of the passage of this Act, the successor National Bank of the United States shall commence issuance of all new legal tender obligations of the United States in the form of U.S. Treasury bills ..."

Section 4. Section 14 of the Federal Reserve Act of 1913 is hereby amended to read: "... Upon the endorsement of any U.S.-chartered bank, any branch of the National Bank may discount up to 50% of the face value of notes, drafts, and bills of exchange arising from the production of tangible wealth or capital improvements....

"Any national bank branch may discount the full value of acceptances which are based on the exportation of goods, or 50% of the value of acceptances which are based on the importation of goods, provided that such goods conform to the restrictions set forth in the preceding paragraphs."

pation credit for medium- to long-term loan capital for hard-commodity production investment and production operating capital or export credit.

And in 1992, Lyndon LaRouche proposed the Federal Reserve Nationalization Act. This particular act lays out precisely how the Treasury Department can take over the Federal Reserve, and then issue this fiat credit through the banking system of the United States—all the private banks would become charter banks of this system—and then the banks would put up part of the loans in order to be able to use the credit extended by the federal government.

The concept of capital account is crucial. In other words, *we're not talking about deficit spending*. We're talking about issuing the currency notes specifically for productive investment. And Lyndon LaRouche has, in many locations, specified the kinds of productive investments which would have access to such credit. If you're investing productively in infrastructure, in nuclear power plants, in water management, you're creating real wealth in the economy which will allow you to repay that credit. For instance, if you're going to be building mass transit, maglev trains in this country, that will mean you're going to have to have subcontractors, who are going to be producing steel. That means many people will be employed in highly skilled, high-paid jobs.

The objective, in other words, should not just be that we're going to return auto plants to this country. We can also use the machine-tool capacity of this country to produce tractors for export to Africa. We can use those machine tools to produce maglev trains. There are all sorts of things that we can do through this process. The idea Lyndon LaRouche puts forward (this was in 1992,—perhaps you'd want to have more credit than he proposed back then—but at that point, he talked about $1 trillion a year being extended in credit for these kinds of productive investments), is that this would create six million new jobs, in goods production, manufacturing, and infrastructure development.

This is not only what we will need for the United States, to build up our infrastructure here, but because these credits could also be made available for export, that is, for capital goods production in this country, for export to third world countries This would be the basis for the United States working together with Russia, China, India, and other countries in a New Bretton Woods arrangement, in which you have agreements in terms of credit extension, to joint sponsorship of projects throughout the entire world. That was the vision of Franklin Roosevelt, for the post–World War II period— and that means more jobs in the United States. As long as you're ensuring that these investments are in productive areas, as opposed to building casinos and other such nonproductive areas, then you're laying the basis for being able to repay the credit extended—either by the country which is importing the export goods from us, because they will then have a more productive economy which will allow them to repay the credit extended; but also, the same is true domestically, because the productivity of the workforce will increase, as well as increased tax revenue through productive investment.

No Alternative to Victory

This is the element which, at the moment, is missing in President Trump's conception of the "American model," or the American System. It is the Gordian Knot of today which must be untied. And the means for doing that is precisely what Lyndon LaRouche has put forward.

Where are we now? We're in the midterms. We have about 23 days left before the elections. These elections are extraordinarily important, particularly in terms of preventing the Democrats from initiating impeachment proceedings and moving forward with the British coup against the Presidency, which would paralyze this country completely. We're in a situation in which much of the population is whipsawed on the basis of the news cycle and momentary developments.

Our intervention in this election is intended to shape the Presidency, shape the policy of this country, and to bring about a new era on this planet, which the President has an intention to do, but for which he needs further guidance which we, through the work of Lyndon LaRouche, are offering him, the American citizens, and the leaders of other nations throughout the world. This is the only way out of the crisis which we're facing today. I'll close with a quote from LaRouche, from an article he wrote in 2005, "The Global Option for this Emergency: Beyond Westphalia Now":

> It can be done, but it could be done only under the pressures of a global crisis as immediately menacing as the situation now. Necessity will be the forceful mother of the needed invention. Nations will swim in the waters of a new economic system, not because of a zeal for swimming, but because they perceive that it is necessary to swim, if one is to survive.

National Sovereignty and a New Bretton Woods

by Robert Ingraham

Oct. 11—World-wide, a growing discussion is now emerging as to the instability which is unfolding within the global system of world finance and banking. Many individuals are now speaking of the unsustainability of existing debt burdens, of the dramatic weakness of many national currencies, and of domestic credit bubbles, such as those of student loans and real estate valuation. Some observers are warning of a repeat of the crisis and crash of 2007-2008. A more astute minority point to the continuing cancer of global derivatives trading and speak of a crisis far worse than what occurred a decade ago.

EIRNS/Sylvia Rosas

LaRouche PAC organizing near the Cliffside Park Post Office in New Jersey, May 14, 2019.

Recognition of the escalating crisis is becoming acute, and many individuals in government, business and academia are now putting forward proposals for financial and banking reforms. There are efforts underway in several nations to implement some form of Glass-Steagall "bank separation"; there is much talk about resolving the problem of "too big to fail banks"; and other piecemeal proposals have been put forward.

Amidst all this nervous and alarmist hand-wringing, however, what is most interesting, what is revelatory, is what is not being discussed. The vacant chair at the dinner table gives the game away. What is absent from almost all the current proposals—both those well-intentioned and those one might term deliberately sophist—is any recognition of, or willingness to address, the underlying self-destructive axioms of the financial system itself.

Only the LaRouche Political Action Committee (LPAC) and this publication have stated categorically that nothing less than a return to the pre-1971 system of "fixed exchange rates" is required. Only LPAC and *EIR* have insisted that the only way to prevent a global financial blow-out is to convene a New Bretton Woods Monetary Conference and to return to the economic and monetary philosophy of Franklin Roosevelt, circa 1942-1945.

Many "experts" dismiss LPAC's proposal out of hand. Others despair that such an agreement were impossible at this time, given the tension in relations between the United States, China, Russia, India and the EU. Many observers simply sigh and assert, "You can't put the toothpaste back in the tube." They insist that all efforts at "reform" must be made within the axioms of the current system. They demand that the "independence" of the financial markets is sacrosanct, and that the power that has been accumulated in the last 40-odd years in the City of London, Wall Street and the unregulated "off-shore" banks—as well is in the appendages of this system, such as the IMF and WTO—is untouchable.

It is self-evident that when one considers the upper echelon of the City of London, its violent objections to a New Bretton Woods agreement flow from geopolitical, Malthusian and imperial motives. But what about the many others who defend the current speculative financial system, those who do not harbor a willful anti-human agenda? Are their concerns merely of a "practical" nature—or is there a deeper phenomenon, something "beneath the floorboards" which must be considered? Are there axiomatic assumptions built into our post-1971 culture which are at play here? That is the question we shall examine in this report.

A Culture Governed by Fortuna

In speaking about his years as a business consultant, Lyndon LaRouche would often state that when he was called in to help fix an ailing company, what was most important were not the reports he was given on the company, but what was not reported. Similarly, in looking at how elected officials, business leaders, the news media and the general public view financial and monetary policy today, how they discuss it, and the solutions they put forward—one item is almost never mentioned:

In 1971, Richard Nixon terminated the gold-reserve monetary system, abandoned fixed exchange-rates between nations, and abolished the post-World War II Bretton Woods System. That is now 47 years ago. What this means is that anyone today who is, say, younger than 60 years old, grew to maturity and has lived the entirety of his or her adult life within a financial system which is literally based on gambling. The casino-like axioms of this system are now fixed in the mind of the citizenry as "how things are"—they have never known anything else. This has profoundly affected what they think about every facet of economics and finance. In a certain way, we might say that many of our fellow citizens have adopted an oligarchical view of economics.

This is even observable among some who support Glass-Steagall and other features of FDR's approach. They see the crisis, they see the need for reform, yet their view is from the bottom-up, never rising to the level of challenging the axioms of the current system itself. Their approach to the current crisis is like a plumber trying to fix a leaky faucet while the tsunami wave approaches from the beach.

The crippling injury which has been inflicted upon our culture is tantamount to a mental harness, preventing individuals from perceiving and acting upon readily available solutions to this crisis. What actually exists

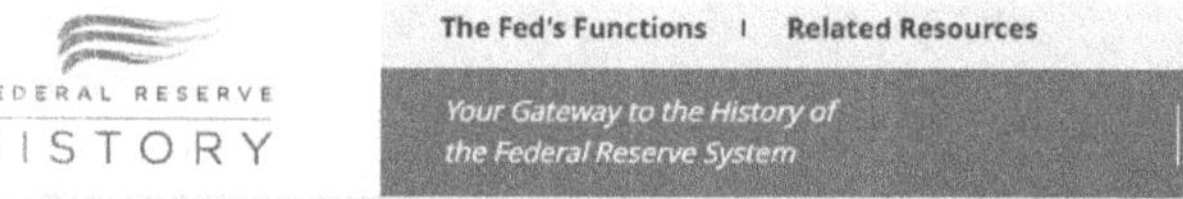

Nixon Ends Convertibility of US Dollars to Gold and Announces Wage/Price Controls

August 1971

With inflation on the rise and a gold run looming, President Richard Nixon's team enacted a plan that ended dollar convertibility to gold and implemented wage and price controls, which soon brought an end to the Bretton Woods System.

Richard Nixon Library

President Richard Nixon at his press conference announcing the end of convertibility of the dollar to gold, thus beginning the end of the FDR's Bretton Woods international monetary system.

today is a widespread shared delusion as to the nature of economy, money and wealth, a delusion which permeates our culture and is particularly pernicious among those policy-makers in Congress and the legacy news media who attempt to control the nation's future.

The Merriam-Webster Dictionary defines "delusion" as "something that is falsely or delusively believed or propagated" and as "a persistent, false psychotic belief regarding the self or persons or objects outside the self that is maintained despite indisputable evidence to the contrary." It should be noted that a delusion is a serious mental illness, literally a psychosis, and as such, any approach to treating it falls within the field of psychopathology. As with Doctor Tarr and Professor Fether, the inmates have been running the asylum for some time now, and only an uncompromising approach, one which insists on truth and historical accuracy, can right this state of affairs.

The current axioms and economic beliefs must be shattered, and the patient must be cured. Hopefully, a few lessons from history will aid in that recovery process.

The Renaissance Created Modern Economics

In his recent speech to the UN General Assembly, President Donald Trump's primary theme emphasized his highly laudable commitment to a revival of a world based on the inviolable principle of national sovereignty. Unfortunately, in the post-1971 world, most of today's leading economists are at a loss to find any connection between the sovereignty of individual nation states and the principles upon which beneficial economic systems are based.

What has been lost in our culture is any lawful understanding as to how human society and human economy was advanced, and what interventions made such advances possible. In truth, throughout the long history of the human species, most societies have been governed by oligarchies, and the oligarchical systems of those elites have always been to the benefit of the few and the exploitation of the many. This was the sad state of human affairs in Europe and the Mediterranean region for thousands of years.

What changed this, what unleashed a new power for human advancement was the invention of the sovereign nation state in the 15th century, an invention which flowed from the Renaissance concept of the *Commonwealth*, as it was developed by Cardinal Nicholas of Cusa and his allies.

In 1461 Louis XI ascended the throne of France and proceeded to establish the first modern, sovereign nation-state. He created a national currency. He built ports, roads, schools, industry, and infrastructure. He authored a work, *Le Rosier des Guerres* (The Rosebush of Wars), wherein he defines that all economic policy must be grounded in a commitment to the "Common Good," for present and future generations. And he established that all economic policy toward that goal, falls under the proper sovereign authority of the nation-state.

In 1485, Henry Tudor overthrew the degenerate Venice-allied Plantagenet dynasty in England, and as King Henry

King Louis XI of France (1423-1483)

Master of the Life of the Virgin
Nicholas of Cusa (1401-1464)

Portrait by Anon.
King Henry VII of England (1457-1509)

VII, he adopted the same methods of national economic development and sovereignty that Louis had pursued in France.

These actions began modern economics, and they defined the inseparable link between sovereignty and progressive economic development. A significant mental block we face today, is that many people are brainwashed into thinking that "national sovereignty" defines a world of "nation vs. nation," whereas the Renaissance principle of *Commonwealth*—sovereignty as understood by Louis XI or Henry VII—is *sovereignty over oligarchy*, i.e., that a sovereign nation recognizes no external or internal oligarchical or financial power over its own sovereign power to print money, define credit policy, regulate banking, or to take whatever actions are required to advance the productive powers of the nation. This is precisely the concept contained within the command to "protect and defend the General Welfare," as defined in the United States Constitution.

Roots of Today's Dilemma

Unprecedented human progress flowed from the effects of the 15th Century Renaissance and the creation of the first sovereign nations. The European oligarchy recognized the threat that sovereignty and upward progress represented to their interests, and they acted against it. First, from Venice, but then from Amsterdam and London, they deployed to create a new form of monetary and financial empire. They could not prevent the emergence of nations, so they acted to subjugate nations to a supra-national system of oligarchical banking and finance, one which they dictated was outside the power of nations to control.

This notion of the supremacy of private financial power over the sovereign nation is the secret to what occurred in

Bernard de Mandeville (1670-1733)

John Locke (1632-1704)

authorized the issuance of sovereign U.S. currency (Greenbacks), as a Constitutional measure, to finance the war effort.

Oligarchical 'Money' and Finance

One of the excretions of the Amsterdam/London oligarchical laboratory in the 17th and 18th centuries was the invention of "central bank money," i.e., that the "governments" of Britain and the Netherlands handed over to the oligarchical Bank of England and Bank of Amsterdam the monopoly right to issue currency. The private banknotes of these institutions were then used to capitalize the London and Amsterdam stock exchanges.

The stock exchanges themselves were built around the buying and selling of the stocks of the "Big 5" companies: the British East India Company, the Dutch East India Company, the Dutch West India Company, the Bank of England itself, and the South Sea Company. Simultaneously, these companies produced huge profits through the looting and exploitation of subject peoples in Asia, Africa and the Americas, exploitation which included total British and Dutch domination of the global trade in both slaves and narcotics.

It is from these cannibalistic practices that Adam Smith developed his theory of monetary "wealth." All of this was grounded in an extreme notion of "monetarism," of independently existing "money"—actually money created by the oligarchs' private banks— magically moving the levers of trade and investment. New industry, new breakthroughs in science and technology, advances in human productivity—none of these have a place

Amsterdam and London in the 17th and 18th centuries. This supremacy of the financial oligarchy has been the continuing species-nature of the British Empire to the present day. In practice, nations are allowed limited sovereignty over certain practical matters, but the purse strings and financial power sit in London, or one of its allied appendages.

Apologists and propagandists for imperial rule, such as Bernard de Mandeville, John Locke and Adam Smith, defended this oligarchical agenda by cloaking it in the guise of "freedom," and to this day that fraudulent characterization is still repeated *ad nauseam*, particularly by those who are devotees of the British-sponsored Austrian School of economics.

Benjamin Franklin, George Washington and Alexander Hamilton were wiser. They understood that sovereignty was meaningless unless it encompassed absolute national sovereignty over financial, banking and monetary policy. Abraham Lincoln understood this also. When London-allied New York banks attempted to blackmail his incoming administration and to bankrupt the U.S. government into subservience, Lincoln shut down the Gold Room in New York and

Adam Smith (1723-1790)

Portrait by Joseph Duplessis
Benjamin Franklin (1706-1790)

Portrait by Charles Willson Peale
George Washington (1732-1799)

George Peter Alexander Healy, 1858
John Quincy Adams

in Smith's schema. They are to be disregarded, or if the oligarchical master demands, to be prevented. Only monetary wealth is allowed as a measurement.

This is the monstrosity which the American colonists rebelled against in 1775, and it still defines the evil we face today. None of these oligarchical practices, nor the theories of Smith and his ilk, have anything to do with defending the Common Good, building the nation-state, or advancing human progress.

The abolition of the Bretton Woods System in 1971—an event only made possible with the murder of John F. Kennedy eight years before—signaled a return to world-rule by the financial oligarchy. The post-1971 floating exchange rate system—which still exists today—represents a total surrender of the sovereign power of governments to control their own currencies. Today's London-based oligarchy seeks to dictate financial policy and to advance its own interests, just as it tried to do (unsuccessfully) with Abraham Lincoln in 1861,

and just as the British East India Company tried to force tea on Boston in 1775.

Hamilton's Vision

One of America's greatest presidents, John Quincy Adams, defined America's global mission as promoting a "Community of Principle" among sovereign nation-states. Is this not what Franklin Roosevelt intended with his Good Neighbor policy? Was this not the original intent of FDR's Bretton Woods agreements? Is this not what has been destroyed in the post-1971 era of globalization and unregulated predatory finance? Is this not what a revived New Bretton Woods System—one based on cooperative and mutually beneficial relations among sovereign nations—will make possible once again?

The very idea that we live in an unregulated "global marketplace," wherein governments are subject to the whims and greed of private financial interests, is anathema to the principles of the U.S. Declaration of Independence and the U.S.

wikipedia
Alexander Hamilton

Constitution. It is also a delusion. Adam Smith's "invisible hand" is the omnipresent claw of the oligarchy reaching into your pocket. There is no "free market"—as in Las Vegas, the house sets the rules. Behind the World Trade Organization, the International Monetary Fund and such abominations as the Intergovernmental Panel on Climate Change, stands the power of a financial oligarchy determined to stop human progress and prohibit the exercise of national sovereignty.

We have seen the results of this rigged game again and again in Asia, Africa, and Latin America, as well as within the European Union. Nations are forced into usurious debt traps, raw materials are looted at give-away prices, and "raids" are conducted on national currencies, to brow-beat governments into submission. It is entirely a murderous, predatory system, one in which the vast majority of humanity is reduced to the perpetual status of underdogs, seeking merely to survive.

Alexander Hamilton has given us the way out from this hellish system. Hamilton's U.S. Constitution resurrected the Renaissance principle of the *Commonwealth*, as is explicit in that document's *Preamble*. The *impulse to develop*, which is implicit in the concept of a Commonwealth—and is inseparable from the true nature of human society—forms the basis for Hamilton's argument in his *Report on Manufactures*, wherein continued human progress, which results from human scientific and technological creation, is made the responsibility of government. The means to achieve this are fully discussed in his Reports on Public Credit and a National Bank. All of this rests on a foundation of absolute national sovereignty.

Mandatory in our Constitution is that no one— either domestic or foreign—has the authority to coin or print money, or to determine how such money will be put into circulation and usage, other than the nation's sovereign government. Despite what the British oligarchs want people to believe, money has no independent existence. All money is Constitutional money and is issued as a form of credit by the nation's government for the purpose of "protecting and promoting the General Welfare" for present and future genera-

LaRouche defeated Prof. Abba Lerner (center) in the celebrated Dec. 2, 1971 Queens College debate.

tions. Any other notion or usage of money is unconstitutional.

LaRouche's Time

It is precisely the recognition of this awesome power of sovereign government which forms the basis for the proposals made by Lyndon LaRouche in his 2014 "The Four New Laws to Save the U.S.A. Now!," as well as in LaRouche's 1998 formal proposal for the creation of a New Bretton Woods Monetary System.

LaRouche's fight to defend the principle of upward human progress is now more than 50 years in duration. Over the course of these long decades, he has been slandered, ostracized and imprisoned for his courage. In the Autumn of 1971, in a debate with the proto-fascist Social-Democrat economist Abba Lerner, LaRouche correctly identified that the abandonment of the Bretton Woods system would lead directly into economic policies of looting and mass murder, modeled on Nazi Germany. In the years since that now fully vindicated forecast, LaRouche has again and again enunciated the pathway to economic recovery for America and the rest of the world. We have now reached a moment in time when LaRouche's proposals are not only correct, but their realization is imminently possible.

America's historic mission is incomplete. We have not yet succeeded in winning the war against the oligarchy. Today's joyful discovery is that in completing the job begun in 1775, we shall also accomplish the solution to the current financial and economic crisis that threatens the planet.

South Dakota Congressional Candidate Wieczorek Hosts Tri-State Meeting, Backing a New 'Just' World System

by Marcia Merry Baker and Jason Ross

Oct. 16—Ron Wieczorek, Independent candidate for South Dakota's single Congressional seat in Washington, held a campaign event on Sunday, October 14, in Sioux Falls, bringing together thirty engaged participants from South Dakota, Minnesota, Iowa, and beyond for a day-long series of briefings, presentations, and dialogue. Candidate Wieczorek stated in his welcoming remarks, "Every crisis we face—war, drugs, the farm crisis, energy, health care, income, disaster protection—is related to an unjust system. Thank God there's a new system coming out of the Pacific," referring to the Belt and Road Initiative (BRI) development corridors now spreading across Eurasia, Africa, and into South America. The conference was organized to present a full picture of this, as the necessary context for taking up what must be done in the United States and the Americas. Wieczorek identified the "British free trade system" as the enemy of mankind.

Among the event attendees were several volunteers who had helped Wieczorek achieve ballot status for the Nov. 6 election, for which he filed nearly 4,000 signatures in April. Farming and ranching were the principal occupations of the assembled guests, whose familiarity with physical production and technological improvement allowed a high-level discussion of what Wieczorek refers to as "moral economics," and the LaRouche method.

Wieczorek himself, 75 years old, has a solid background in productive agriculture, as does his family, going back generations. His experience includes operat-

Robert Baker

Ron Wieczorek, Independent candidate for South Dakota's statewide Congressional district, speaks at his Oct. 14 campaign policy conference in Sioux Falls, titled, "Family Farms in Biggest Ever Crash, Need Biggest Ever Solution: American System Emergency Measures for the Whole Economy; 'New Bretton Woods' for World Development."

ing and selling farm machinery, interstate custom harvesting, and today, raising Charolais bulls. Since the late 1980s, when he first encountered the international policy work of Lyndon and Helga Zepp-LaRouche's newly-formed Schiller Institute Food-for-Peace drive—founded in Chicago in September 1988—and at large, Wieczorek has led the charge for what he stresses is a new, moral economic system. For the last eight months, Wieczorek has campaigned hard with this message, making use of various high-profile means to get his word out.

He has criss-crossed the state addressing various constituency organizations, for example the South Dakota Stock Growers Association (cattle, sheep) in Rapid City, the South Dakota Veterans Council/American Legion in Sioux Falls, the Farmers Union in Delmont, and the Downtown Rotary Club in Sioux Falls.

He has participated in a number of debates with the three other candidates, including at the Dakotafest fair in Mitchell, the KSFY-TV sponsored debate at the State Fairgrounds in Huron, the Americans for Prosperity—South Dakota forum in Sioux Falls, and a candidates'

Candidate Ron Wieczorek (standing, left) addresses a point in the discussion during a presentation by Bob Baker (at podium) during the ten-hour dialogue, attended by some thirty people in the course of the day.

forum sponsored by the Concerned Citizens of Fall River County in Hot Springs.

He has been interviewed and covered by radio, television and print media throughout the state, including the *Lakota Country Times*, "the only official legal South Dakota Indian newspaper on Tribal Land," with a circulation of over 80,000 to all Native American reservations in the upper Midwest.

Ron, his wife Deanna, his two sisters, and other campaign volunteers have maintained high visibility in local communities and on college campuses, driving their Wieczorek for Congress "float" (a pick-up truck) in the many fall homecoming parades. Every day, Ron and volunteers are stopping off in dozens of farm towns, at their convenience store/gas stations, the last remaining social centers in rural counties. Tens of thousands of Ron's programmatic flyers are circulating this way throughout the state.

South Dakota has only one Federal Congressman, since its population is below a million. Nearly half live in Sioux Falls, in the southeast corner, near to Minnesota, Iowa and Nebraska. By now, most of the residents, as well as through-drivers, have come to know Ron through his huge, lighted campaign billboard on Interstate 90 just east of Sioux Falls. Their common response is that they love the part that says, "Jail Wall Street." It advertises electing Wieczorek, and implementing "LaRouche's Four Economic Laws."

The World Silk Road

The Sioux Falls conference on October 14 was a marathon of discussion, running the gamut from the present-day strategic crisis to LaRouche's philosophical and historical method; from past history to proposals for the future. LaRouche associates Bob Baker, Marcia Merry Baker, and Jason Ross came in from out-of-state, to provide illustrated presentations on the following themes: a world tour of the Belt and Road Initiative; LaRouche's history of organizing for a new world economic system; mega-projects (both planned and underway) in China, the Mideast and Africa, Southeast Asia, and the Americas; the British Empire system as the enemy of mankind; the nature of discovery and how to organize education with the goal of fostering creativity; LaRouche's Four Laws; environmentalism as an anti-human fraud; and the beautiful nature of the human species, made in the image of God.

Bach and Handel piano music called the assembly together, and at day's end, in celebration, all joined in singing "The Battle Hymn of the Republic."

Throughout the day, most prominent among Ron Wieczorek's responses to questions and discussion was his view of the central importance of adopting a personal mission. When a long-time activist farmer expressed dismay at the difficulty of achieving the needed political changes, Ron responded forcefully: "The problem isn't what's going on out there; it's what's going on between your ears." Intervening at another moment of overwhelmed recognition of the magnitude of the tasks we have assigned ourselves, Wieczorek expressed the solution in one word: "Outreach!" He declared, "We have to defeat immoral economics."

How Do You Know What Is True?

One highlight of the day's discussion arose from by Jason Ross's presentation on the primacy of the concept of discovery itself in LaRouche's economic method. Against the background of our species' ability to create resources and expand our numbers through mastery of physical principles, Ross posed the dilemma: Many concepts that seem almost self-evident to us and are taken for granted, have a basis unknown to us. For example, we all think we know that the Earth is a sphere, but how many could help an eight-year-old understand why we know it? After a discussion of Eratosthenes, the audience was surprised by Ross's remark that on the Earth, it is impossible to draw a square, and that an east-west line cannot be straight!

This led to a report on surveying by Minnesota farm leader Andy Olson, who has noticed that at the edges of counties, the roads and power line tracks that are supposed to be "straight," actually bend. This can be seen in the surveying done in the Western lands for the 1860s Homestead Act, and in Minnesota, and on the checkerboard of square "sections" throughout the Plains. Working through these conundrums together was a direct social experience of creative thought.

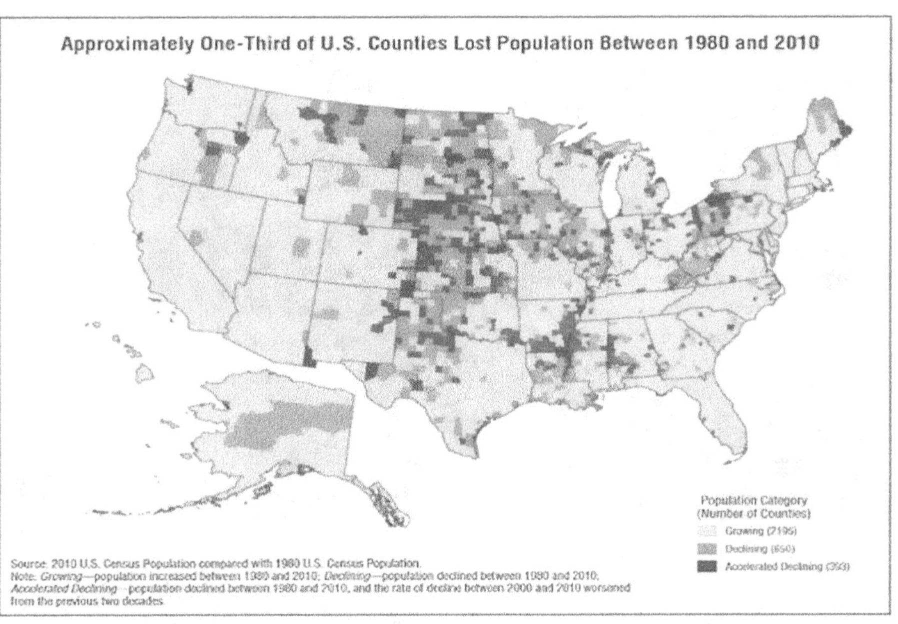

The thirty-year pattern of population loss, shown here by county, is severe in the Farmbelt, concentrated in the High Plains. It has intensified over the last eight years.

The same depth of dialogue took place around LaRouche's key concept of energy flux-density. Ross presented the history of energy in terms of the "gift of fire" to mankind by Prometheus and historical advances in the forms and quality of "fire." Bob Baker conveyed the concept of energy flux-density in his presentation of "The Astronaut Farmer." He demonstrated the "powering up" of the human hand through technological advances in three areas of farming: tilling, seeding, and harvesting.

Together, these topics allowed the concept to come to life, and sparked a fiery discussion about whether an increase of the productive powers of labor could go *too far*, having the effect in the farmbelt of ever larger, more powerful, satellite-driven machinery, acting to depopulate rural areas to the point that the noetic field of knowledgeable farmers could become too diffuse. The average age of farmers is, in fact, rising. The countryside of productive farmsteads and family-scale farming is shutting down, in favor of plantation-scale agriculture.

Why the Depopulation?

Several farmers took the occasion to report on the devastation they personally witness on a daily basis: Once thriving local towns are now boarded up, or even being bulldozed flat; once lively farmsteads dotting the landscape amidst the fields, are either gone or just a sole dwelling surrounded by decaying out-buildings.

This led to a heated discussion of how sovereign government policy can intervene to stop this devolution, by making crucial decisions about what scale of farming to foster, with measures that are known to work: parity pricing, production management, ending mega-monopolies, use of the Commodity Credit Corporation (set up in the FDR period), and most importantly, re-asserting national sovereignty over farm, manufacturing, infrastructure-building and, indeed, all economic policy.

A young Iowa farm leader put forward concrete ideas for improving the farmbelt under an economic system suited to production: re-instate Glass-Steagall and use Federal government powers for production management. For example, by setting up beneficial set-aside programs when needed, initiating parity pricing, and engaging in anti-trust actions. To answer the usual counter-argument, that parity farm commodity pricing will hurt consumers by driving up prices, this cattleman has done work-ups of how this can be done. He told the meeting there must be a transition to restoring productive organization in rural areas, and it can be done to the benefit of all.

Marcia Merry Baker also hit on this task, in giving a report on "The Americas," covering the dismal picture of both the economic decline and lack of infrastructure in North America in the last half century, in contrast to

Robert Baker

Minnesota roundtable discussion Oct. 12 in Morgan (near Minneapolis), hosted by Redwood County Councilman Bob Van Hee (standing, left) joined by Gene Schenk (standing, center) on the "Farm/U.S. Economy Crisis—the Need for the American System and a 'New Bretton Woods.'" Seated front left is Jason Ross of the LaRouche PAC science team, who spoke, along with Bob Baker and Marcia Merry Baker.

what we know should be undertaken: connectivity through a continental, high-speed rail grid; infrastructure to defend against disasters, such as flooding, fires, high-wind events, and earthquakes; and providing new supplies of fresh water for the western drylands. There are initiatives for this, in league with the BRI, in Central and South America.

Moreover, there is no need—in a developing world where we look forward to the African continent becoming food self-sufficient, and all other regions likewise—for the Americas, both North and South, to remain the soybean monoculture source areas for the globe, a situation in which the Bunges, Cargills, Dreyfuses, and other cartels obtain their commodities dirt-cheap, just to turn around and use this food capacity to swindle farmers and enforce hunger. This must end, and we can do it. Mrs. Baker provided exact quotes from the 1988 UN General Agreement on Tariffs and Trade (GATT) Montreal Round, when the U.S. delegation, headed by former Cargill Vice President Daniel Amstutz, for the first time ever, said U.S. policy no longer supports food self-sufficiency. As of then, the United States supported obtaining food on the "world market"—classic British "free" trade, for our national food supply.

Bob Baker and Jason Ross gave hard-hitting presentations on the British pedigree of the enemy of development: the spider web of subversive globalist finance; the insane lies of the "green" genocide

movement; the danger of British imperial geopolitics agitating for a world war. There were "amens" from the audience, on the way that President Trump is standing up to the British attack job being run so obviously through the Russiagate hoax, and all the other filthy operations. Trump's friendship diplomacy initiatives with the leaders of Russia, China, Japan, India and other nations are the way out of the British system era, and into a new, better future for humanity.

The Minnesota Meeting

Two days earlier, on Friday, October 12, in Morgan, Minnesota (in Redwood County, southwest of Minneapolis) eighteen farm community leaders gathered to discuss the same world picture and urgent political tasks, at a roundtable meeting hosted by County Board Commissioner Robert Van Hee.

Here again, the first comment by one farmer was, "How do we stop this terrible depopulation?" They spoke of how drug running, drug use and drug deaths are all over the place. Several participants at this meeting, and also at the Wieczorek campaign conference, first became active policy fighters thirty years ago, when Lyndon and Helga LaRouche first convened the Schiller Institute Food-for-Peace effort for strategic change all across the board.

Prominent among those early recruits to the movement was Gene Schenk, originally from Minnesota, who was now back on home ground, attending both the Redwood Falls and Sioux Falls events. Schenk is a communications volunteer for Ron's South Dakota campaign.

Wieczorek's initiative has not only mobilized endorsements in South Dakota for his candidacy for federal office, but has catalyzed a broader mobilization throughout the farmbelt for more organized discussion and leadership to shift national practices and policies.

marciabaker@larouchepub.com
jasonaross@gmail.com

ZEPP-LAROUCHE WEBCAST

The Stakes in the U.S. Midterm Elections: War or Peace

This is the edited transcript of the Schiller Institute's October 11, 2018 New Paradigm webcast with the founder of the Schiller Institutes, Helga Zepp-LaRouche. She is interviewed by Harley Schlanger. A video *of the webcast is available.*

Harley Schlanger: Hello, I'm Harley Schlanger with the Schiller Institute. Welcome to our webcast for Oct. 11, 2018. Our webcast today will feature, as always, Helga Zepp-LaRouche, our founder and Chairwoman.

Helga and I were just reviewing events prior to this webcast. There's so much going on as we come now with less than five weeks to the midterm elections in the United States, which will be extraordinarily important in determining whether the American people are going to step up to the responsibility of joining the New Paradigm, or whether they're going to succumb to the demoralization and the media control.

Jitters on Wall Street: a New Great Depression?

We're also seeing things that the LaRouche movement is famous for: economic forecasting. Helga, why don't we start with that? We saw a very big drop in the stock market yesterday; there's jitters on Wall Street, anxiety around the world. What's going on?

Helga Zepp-LaRouche: The system is disintegrating, and it's just a question of time when this will happen. I find it very remarkable that the IMF is pronouncing the famous "D" word. Remember that the "D"

word was never to be mentioned, because the market would supposedly follow the psychology of the markets, and when you mention the word "Depression," then that could bring it on, so went the tale. But now the IMF meeting in Bali, Indonesia is warning that challenges are to be faced, otherwise, the second Great Depression would be looming.

Now, I find this really remarkable, and I think they're trying to somehow prepare the population that the thing is really coming down. This stock market plunge of more than 800 points—I think something like 820—you had President Trump who basically said the Federal Reserve is "crazy" with their interest rate policy, which caused a strong reaction by IMF Managing Director Christine Lagarde and so forth, but he kept on, repeating it twice. He said the situation is much too tense to continue. This is the

Organizing for LaRouche's Four Laws at a LaRouche PAC literature table in New York City in 2018.

EIRNS/Sylvia Spaniolo

reason why you have the reverse carry trade from the emerging markets, which was mentioned by the IMF as the biggest threat to the system, and the second biggest threat or maybe on an equal level, being the indebtedness. Now, Lagarde also mentioned the indebtedness of the governments, the corporate firms, and also other categories, like student loans and car loans and all of this, is 60% higher than it was in 2008.

Then, in addition to all of these things, you have the collapse of the real economy, with for example home-building having peaked in the United States in January and has been in freefall, and since about May this was also the case for copper and timber—all of these have lost between 15 and 20% since the beginning of the year. So, these are all markers that this thing will not continue.

And then, on top of that there is the growing fight between the EU and Italian government. You had the famous letter, or infamous letter by the two EU Commissioners Pierre Moscovici and Valdis Dombrovskis, to the Italian government, warning them that their intention not to stick to the EU-imposed budget deficit of 2.4%, would not be allowed, which triggered a run on the Italian bond, and as a result, the spread between the Italian and the German values have gone up to 300 points; and it is generally said if it goes up to 400— meaning that Italians will have to pay 3% and more to refinance their loans—that could contribute to a crisis.

On top of it, by the 15th of this month, that is, in four days, the Italian government will publish the details of its budget. And it is expecting that the rating agencies will immediately afterwards put out some rating, that in all likelihood downgrades the Italian bonds, or downgrades Italy as a country. Depending on the formulation, if the outlook is basically neutral, people will say this could just pass; but if they put a negative outlook on it, then it could lead to a big banking crisis—actually not only for Italy, but for the entire Western financial system.

It is clear that some people in the European Central Bank and EU Commission think they can force the Italian government to capitulate, that they can control the consequences of this, but they are playing with fire: Because you have a highly, highly volatile financial system, and I can only say, in 2008, the whole world was more or less unprepared for the crash, because they were not listening to the warning my husband had put out, very clearly, July 25, 2007—one week before the secondary mortgage crisis in the United States exploded. And he had said at that time, that this system is finished; all that you can see now, is how it comes down. People didn't listen. So the crash occurred in 2008 and they didn't draw any conclusions out of their own mistakes, and just kept pumping money— quantitative easing. All these instruments of the central banks are now completely exhausted and used up.

And contrary to 2008, when everybody was unprepared, those people who are now trying to cause the Italian government to capitulate and continue with the austerity, while the Italian government was voted in, because it rejected that austerity. So, if they push too hard, I think one should not forget that both Italian government coalition parties, the Lega and the Five Star Movement party, have Glass-Steagall not only in their party programs, but also in their coalition agreement.

Now, obviously, the Italian government knows what they're up against. They have seen speculators moving in on countries, driving them into the ground, so they are relatively careful, and they're not saying anything terribly provocative. But if somebody from the outside pushes them into a crash, I would not exclude the possibility, or I would actually say it's quite probable, that they would implement Glass-Steagall in self-defense.

So the situation is quite different from 2008, and I think the only lesson that one can draw out of all of this, is that we need to amplify our efforts to go for a New Bretton Woods system, which we have a campaign on internationally; we have a petition circulating urging it, signed by many people in the meantime, and I would urge you, our viewers, to sign this petition yourself, get it around, prepare anybody you know—elected officials, mayors, parliamentarians, congressmen—to prepare for Glass-Steagall, and not only that, but the Four Laws of Lyndon LaRouche. Because unless we reorganize this entirely bankrupt financial system in an orderly fashion, the danger is an uncontrolled collapse.

You need a New Bretton Woods system, you need Glass-Steagall, we need to get rid of the casino economy; we have to have credit for the financing of the real economy, and we have to have a new credit system to finance investments on a multinational level among all the countries of this world, to get the world out of this danger of a depression.

So, if the IMF is talking about the danger of a Great Depression, people should take it to heart. Think about what happened in the Great Depression in the 1930s—in the United States it was devastation, but in Europe it was even worse, because it led to fascist movements and that to world wars. So people should not take these things lightly: Get on board with us. Join the Schiller Institute, join our campaign for New Bretton Woods, because that's the only answer one can give to this danger of a looming crash.

Is Austerity the Answer?

Schlanger: I had a chance to read through the Executive Summary of the IMF report, and there were two omissions—they were there in a sense, but they didn't really acknowledge them—both of which your husband was out in front of for many, many years, in dealing with the IMF. On the one hand, it's clear that it's *their* policy which has failed. The austerity regime policy which the IMF is famous for, has never led to any economic development. And secondly, the quantitative easing, the low-interest credit which went into speculation, instead of Glass-Steagall—the IMF was promoting that. And so, the two policies they promoted, they're now admitting have failed. Your thoughts on that, Helga?

Zepp-LaRouche: I think the possibility that the IMF would reform itself verges on zero. A different kind

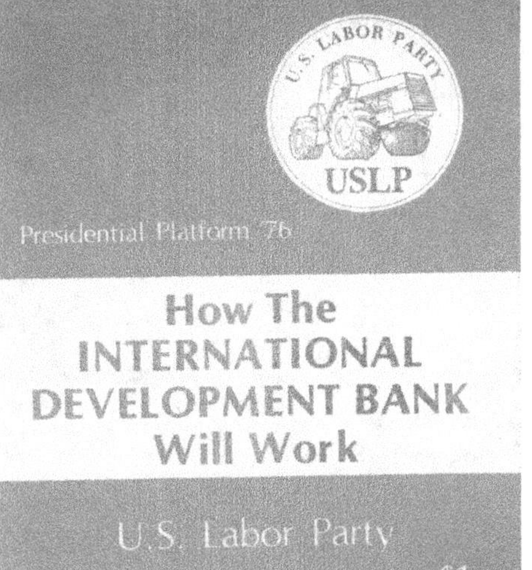

of action is required. In a certain sense, you have right now in the whole world, already, a revolt against these failed neo-liberal policies. This was expressed in the Brexit vote; this was expressed in the election victory of President Trump; the new Italian government is an expression of that; also the new Austrian government.

In a certain sense, national sovereignty has to be reasserted, and these supranational institutions were the main reason these policies were imposed, which created havoc. Look at what happened to Greece. The Greek economy was diminished by one-third. The Italian economy was destroyed. The fact that we have now a totally different government in Italy, which is pro-growth for the most part, which is for good relations with China, for a positive relationship with the New Silk Road—all of this is a response to the failure of these policies. And there are many people in Europe who are expecting that, given the fact that the EU is basically doing exactly the same thing in principle, namely, sticking to the neo-liberal austerity, that you will have an earthquake in the coming European Parliament elections in April, which will mean that these present policies will be absolutely out.

LaRouche's International Development Bank

I think this is much too long term, however. I think the crisis is upon us now, so I can only say that the only solution is the package I just said: The IMF is really a bankrupt organization, as was stated by my husband in 1975, when he proposed to replace this IMF with an International Development Bank, which would provide large-scale, low-interest credit for development projects in the developing sector. If that would have been done, we would not have a migration problem, we would have prosperous countries around the globe. Now, with the New Silk Road, this policy is on a good path.

So I can only say, "Listen to the wise words of Lyndon LaRouche," belatedly, but better late than never.

Schlanger: Lyndon LaRouche's pamphlet, "How the International Development Bank Will Work," was a very popular item back in 1975 when he wrote it.

We used it for his first campaign for President.

Trump: 'The Democrats Have Gone Wacko'

On the upcoming midterm elections, there's a lot of turmoil that's been unleashed. What's clear is that Hillary Clinton has not learned anything from the results of November 2016. You have civil unrest being built, deliberately, because the Mueller Russiagate story is collapsing. This can become a very dangerous situation. Let's start with what Trump said. Trump said, the Democrats have gone "wacko," and are "too dangerous to govern." I assume you would share that assessment, Helga?

Zepp-LaRouche: If calling for violence is a sign of insanity, then I would agree with him. And it's funny, I was looking at the German media, and they all portray this fight, this very hot situation in the United States, as if it's all just electioneering by Trump—calling the Democrats a "mob." But, it is a fact that Rep. Maxine Waters (D-CA) already some months ago, called on everybody to get into the face of Trump cabinet members, whenever you see them—there were some actually violent incidents; people were not served in restaurants; and also some other Democrats called for people to be "in their faces" of the Trump camp.

And that has created a complete hysteria, which was amplified by the Brett Kavanaugh Supreme Court confirmation case. Even Harvard law professor Alan Dershowitz, a liberal Democrat, denounced Sen. Dianne Feinstein and former Attorney General Eric Holder for saying that Kavanaugh should not be accepted, because this would put into question the legitimacy of the Supreme Court! This is really incredible. Dershowitz then correctly said, forget it, Kavanaugh is now confirmed as a Supreme Court Justice and he will be there for his lifetime; this was due process, and the Democrats should go back to being civilized and not violate all the norms and rules.

This is incredible: I'm not an expert on American constitutional questions, but it seems to me that if the Senate, or some Senators, put into question the legitimacy of the Supreme Court, this will lead to a constitutional crisis, or some kind of a state crisis—if these people are not stopped.

I think they have lost all barriers; they have lost all sense of limit! This is a completely hysterical situation, and I can only say that this is very dangerous. We have

Sen. Rand Paul, R-Ky., leaves a meeting of Senate Republicans on Capitol Hill in Washington on Sept. 26, 2018. (AP Photo/Jacquelyn Martin)

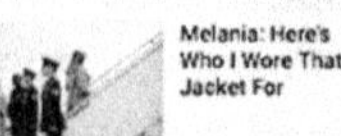

said many times that Trump is being attacked—I mean, you can pick on tiny points here and there, but that's not the point—the attacks are because he is trying to get the U.S. relationship with Russia on a good basis. He had a very successful summit in Helsinki with Putin. And at least, in the initial phase, he had an excellent relationship with China and Xi Jinping. And that is why the geopolitical establishment went absolutely crazy. As a matter of fact, they're escalating their campaign, both against Russia and against China, in unprecedented ways. It is a question of war and peace. People should really understand that, and that the Democrats have really gone crazy on the issue of Russia and also China, and they should not fall into this trap, because the consequence is World War III.

George Soros Funding Rent-a-Mobs

Schlanger: One of the other important points, I think is that what we're seeing, is again, people like George Soros funding these rent-a-mobs. Soros, of course, has been involved in such activity for many, many years. I believe you, Helga, first identified the operation against Trump after the election, as similar to

the "color revolutions" that Soros, combined with people such as Sen. John McCain, the National Endowment for Democracy, and the Clinton State Department, ran throughout the former Soviet bloc countries. I think we're now seeing that what you said about the "color revolution" is totally accurate, including the danger of a Maidan Square-type chaos being unleashed. Sen. Rand Paul said yesterday that he fears that there could be assassinations.

Is this pretty much what you had seen two years ago, this color revolution scenario?

Zepp-LaRouche: Yes. Whenever you have George Soros involved in such things, the speculation naturally goes in this direction. According to reports, he financed to the tune of $50 million, a private group which was called into being by a "senator," not named, but the individual involved was formerly an aide to Sen. Feinstein. This constituted an outsourcing of the whole Christopher Steele operation to a private group, basically using $50 million, so that it could continue after Steele was officially fired from his liaison with the FBI.

New Revelations on Russiagate

Now, this is incredible. I think this will all come out. Even if it was behind closed doors, nevertheless, what came out in various Fox TV programs and various other revelations following the James Baker testimony, was

that it was Michael Sussman, the lawyer of Hillary Clinton's campaign and the lawyer for the DNC, who was the original trigger for the whole Russiagate affair. I find this absolutely incredible and I can only hope that the American voters draw the proper conclusion, because it means that the Hillary Clinton campaign was involved with a foreign power, namely Great Britain, against her opponent in the election campaign, and then afterwards, basically against an elected President. Now, I don't find this very "democratic," to say the least, to use these kinds of intelligence service methods, "deep state" methods, to work against your own President, who has been democratically elected.

This, in my view, is the biggest scandal, and if all comes out, if all the documents are declassified, I think it will go down as the biggest scandal in American history. That's what's at stake with this midterm election.

Schlanger: Baker, who was legal counsel to Director James Comey and the FBI, in his testimony before a closed Congressional hearing, acknowledged that Sussman gave him the Steele report, which was then incorporated into the original FISA warrant against Trump campaign advisor Carter Page. That just makes clear that all these Democrats who have been protesting what Rep. Devin Nunes did in his House Intelligence Committee, were wrong, were lying; they were trying to cover up the connection between the British, the Clinton campaign, and the FBI.

Pence & Pompeo: Mixed Messages in China

Now, Helga, a couple of other things we need to cover before we finish today: One is the very significant stopover in Beijing by Secretary of State Mike Pompeo. He had just come from North Korea, from what appears to be quite a successful meeting with Kim Jong-un. But when he got to China, it was a slightly different environment, largely because of the moves toward trade war. What happened when Pompeo got to Beijing?

Zepp-LaRouche: This was shortly after Vice President Mike Pence had delivered an absolute diatribe at the Hudson Institute Oct. 4, attacking China in the *worst* possible way. This was taken very badly by the Chinese government and Chinese media, who questioned whether Pence's remarks reflected a shift in the Trump Administration to a totally hostile attitude towards China. When Secretary of State Mike Pompeo arrived in Beijing just a few days afterwards, he reiterated that it is the policy of the United States to have a good relationship with China, that the U.S. agrees with the One China policy, and that the United States is not trying to stop the rise of China. Several Chinese media noted the fact that this was an extremely important statement to come at this moment.

There was one interesting article in the *Global Times* by the American analyst and expert, Clifford Kiracofe, who made the point that there is a clear difference between Pence, who sort of speaks for the "deep state," and Trump, who is trying to change U.S. foreign policy, but is being hamstrung by this crew. Kiracofe basically said the U.S. establishment is unwilling to learn the lesson from what's going on strategically, which is that the world is changing and that a multipolarity already exists.

Now, the significance is not just in Kiracofe's saying this, but that *Global Times*, a paper very close to the Chinese government, is also publishing it. So I think it's

White House

Vice President Mike Pence speaking about the Trump Administration's policies toward China at the Hudson Institute on Oct. 4, 2018.

important that the Chinese are still holding out hope for good relations with the United States, despite the trade war and the escalation coming from ridiculous figures such as the Director of Asia Studies at the Council on Foreign Relations, Elizabeth Economy, who was already on a rampage in 2014, who has now come out with another major piece, accusing China, of all things—I don't need to repeat this stuff. In 2014 I said that Elizabeth Economy obviously has an "economy-class mind" if she says these things, and obviously, she has not improved since.

In any case, I think it's very important that Pompeo was there to set the record straight, because the need to find solutions to the world does require the collaboration among the major powers of the world. Those who are pushing this insane confrontation—like Hillary Clinton did in her recent speech at Oxford University, where she delivered an absolute rant against Russia and Trump—should really not be listened to, at all.

New IPCC Report Crazier than Ever

Schlanger: Another group that shouldn't be listened to, but unfortunately is, is the Intergovernmental Panel on Climate Change (IPCC), which is in the news again, with their so-called "manmade climate change" theories, demanding that carbon dioxide be eliminated from the universe. This goes back to the campaign you waged against the British-backed, German figure, Hans Joachim Schellnhuber, who has been pushing these policies. And now it looks as though this nonsense is going to be thrust as a dagger into the heart of the German auto industry. And it's a good thing that Trump pulled the United States out of the Paris Agreement on climate change. Where is this heading?

Zepp-LaRouche: This IPCC report says that the climate accord reached in Paris in

State Department

Secretary of State Michael Pompeo (second from left), Ambassador to China Terry Branstad (left), and Deputy Assistant Secretary of State for Southeast Asia W. Patrick Murphy meeting with Chinese Politburo Member Yang Jiechi in Beijing, China on Oct. 8, 2018.

John Schellnuber, May 17, 2011.

2015 was not enough, that rather than be satisfied with limiting global temperature to a rise of 2 degrees Celsius, we must limit the rise to only 1.5 degrees Celsius by 2050. This is basically what Schellnhuber put out some years ago with the "great transformation" as he called it—the decarbonization of the world economy, getting rid of nuclear, getting rid of coal, oil, gas, just go to "renewable" energy sources.

It is very, very clear that what my husband has developed in terms of the cohesion and the correlation between energy flux-density in the production process, and the potential relative population density that can be maintained with that energy flux-density, means that the goal Schellnhuber has set forth, that the Earth can only carry one billion people, is what they now want to put back on the agenda. It's a desperate effort by the forces of the Empire against Trump, who has promised to reindustrialize the United States; it's especially against the New Silk Road, against the Belt and Road Initiative, the new spirit which has captured more than 100 countries that are now working within the Belt and Road Initiative to their mutual benefit. It's an effort to throw a monkey wrench into this new dynamic.

But I think it's desperate, I think it's dangerous. I don't think it will work. I don't think that these people will convince China, India, Latin America, Africa, the Asian nations, even some of the European nations, to lie down and die, because this is what that would mean.

It's dangerous anyhow, because you can see that the policy to limit global warming needs a mass hysteria on the CO_2 question. I mean, first of all, we have long debated that the CO_2 emissions are really a minimal factor in climate change. Climate change is taking place, there's no question about it, but as we have documented many times in the past, it has to a very large extent to do

with the position of our Solar System in the Galaxy, and it is long-term cycles from Ice Ages to warming periods, and within that, you have still smaller fluctuations; and this is determining the climate.

So the whole discussion of whether the CO_2 emissions by man are causing these climate changes is just completely absurd. Now, it's very dangerous. You can see brainwashing going on of the population. In Europe, for example, one day after the IPCC put out its quack report, the EU Environment Ministers, meeting on Oct. 9, agreed to cut car and van CO_2 emissions, not by 30% as previously agreed to, but by 35% by 2030, even earlier if possible. The German government, which had initially wanted a 30% reduction, agreed with the EU ministers. It's just crazy.

Now, what will that do? Today, Herbert Diess, Chairman of the Management Board and CEO of Volkswagen, the largest German carmaker, came out and said that if a 35% cut in cars' CO_2 emissions is implemented, this will force a reduction of one-fourth of the VW labor force in ten years, or 100,000 jobs—and that's just one carmaker! Add all the other ones, and you will end up with millions of people going unemployed and the whole industry collapsing! Germany, as an economy, is already on extremely fragile ground because of the exit from nuclear energy, and combined with a push to eliminate coal altogether, this will be the death of Germany as an industrial country. Obviously, we will make a big campaign against that.

Why Not Dump Coal Too?

Poland, for example, is 90% dependent on coal for its electricity production. And if countries such as Poland are forced to cease using coal for electricity production, you will have a populist explosion in the next vote, if not earlier.

So this is all completely crazy, and it should be stated very clearly, that with the presently existing technologies, for a very long time to come, the world's population cannot be maintained without coal. There are safe and modern coal plants which are completely environmentally friendly; but the climate crazies are completely motivated, not by considerations to protect our environment, but by an anti-population attitude.

Global Warming Is Not Science

In 2015, we published a report, *'Global Warming' Scare is Population Reduction, not Science.* In that report, we had the Queen of England and Prince Philip on the cover, because Schellnhuber wants to be addressed all the time as "CBE," Commander of the Order of the British Empire. We documented in that report that these are all British policies. We can see this in this new IPCC report and the anti-CO_2 emission campaign. A German court has now banned older diesel fueled cars in 11 zones of Berlin! The German Association of Craftsmen has said that this means that 50,000 cars of craftsmen will not be allowed to drive in the city, and everybody who needs the services of a craftsman, who needs a new roof, or needs a new pump, or whatever, will not be serviced any more.

None of this has anything to do with real issues: It's mass psychosis, and it's driven by the hedge funds, by Wall Street, because the CO_2 emission trade is quackery: We denounced an emissions trading system in the past, and now, to impose a global carbon tax, which is also what is being pushed, would mean they have again a good weapon against national sovereignty, because once you agree that national economies have to submit to policing of their carbon emissions, "there you go again" in the direction of this globalist eco-fascism.

It's not scientific; it's the opposite. It's oligarchical and it's an effort, really aimed, in my view, primarily against the New Silk Road, but also against Trump, against Germany, and many other countries. So, we should really denounce it. We will soon have a new section on our Schiller Institute website, containing lots of articles, interviews and statements. If you have some scientific contribution to make to this subject, we will publish it on this website as a contribution to a public debate. Because this is really dangerous for the future of civilization.

We have to have the opposite approach: We have to have an optimism about man being able to achieve fusion power, to develop completely new scientific methods for energy, safety, for raw materials security, for space travel. I think we should not get into this scare which is really a tool of the oligarchy to try to stop the development of the people.

Endorsement of Rogers for Congress

Schlanger: Helga, we've gone on a little bit longer than usual, but I think there's one other thing we have to bring up, because we teased it last week, which is endorsements for Independent Congressional candidate Kesha Rogers in Texas. In case people don't know this,

Schiller Institute

Roger Stone (inset) endorsed Kesha Rogers for Congress.

EIRNS/Bryan Barajas

in the last couple of days, two very prominent American Republicans and conservatives—actually, they may not even be Republicans in the "party" sense—but Roger Stone, a longtime friend of Donald Trump, a self-proclaimed "political provocateur," issued a very strong endorsement of Kesha Rogers. And then, Senator Richard Black, a Virginia state senator, who's been very involved in exposing the coup and also exposing the "deep state" operations against Syria, issued a statement endorsing Kesha Rogers. Helga, do you have any thoughts on these two endorsements?

Zepp-LaRouche: I think it's great, and I can also add that a former French Presidential candidate, Jacques Cheminade, also endorsed Kesha Rogers, saying that even though he's not an American, Kesha's campaign has international significance, because she is the flagship against everything that's going wrong in the United States right now. I think we will have more such statements, and I really encourage all of you to come out and support Kesha Rogers, because this is a campaign of national importance and international importance. [Rogers is an Independent running in the 9th CD in Texas against incumbent Democrat Al Green, who promotes impeaching President Trump regardless of whether he has committed a constitutionally defined crime or not.—ed.]

Schlanger: OK, I think that about does it. Until next week, Helga. We'll see you.

Zepp-LaRouche: OK, till next week!

Mike Pence's Dumb Ass Speech on China: When the Cat's Away, the Mice Will Play

by Barbara Boyd

Oct. 9—Mike Pence's October 4 speech on China has received widespread international press coverage as representing a new hardline approach to relationships between the United States and China. It was even characterized in some overcharged quarters as the opening of a "New Cold War," although the speech itself hardly lives up to that inflamed billing. Analysts also should have learned by now that it is Donald Trump who runs American foreign policy, and anything that Mike Pence or his ilk proclaim is subject to very rapid change.

As Pence was delivering his speech, the President was traveling throughout the United States, addressing large rallies in an all-out effort to halt the British-inspired coup against him, which is the actual issue in the 2018 midterm elections. He was also in a life-or-death battle over a seat on the U.S. Supreme

Vice President Mike Pence bashes China at the Hudson Institute in Washington, D.C. on Oct. 4, 2018.

Court—a battle which could determine whether or not the nation itself descends into the sexual McCarthyite madness of the "Me-Too" movement. Many have rightly characterized the battle over the Kavanaugh nomination as a dry run for the battle over impeachment which will be launched if the Democrats win the House.

Pence, along with other old-school tools of the Washington-Wall Street-London neo-con axis, like Nikki Haley, have adopted a strategy toward the President which involves endless self-preening, unabashed flattery, and feigned loyalty. For that, both have earned the moniker "toadies in chief" from the legacy U.S. news media. Their sycophantic fawning conceals the naked ambition of their own Presidential aspirations. Pence believes that he was ordained by God to become President of the United States. Both Haley and

Director of National Intelligence Dan Coats.

U.S. Ambassador to the UN Nikki Haley.

The British Have Overplayed Their Hand   33

Pence have a history of working aggressively to undermine Trump's most significant initiatives, in this case, Trump's relationship with China's President Xi Jinping.

For that, both Pence and Haley have rightly earned the speculation in Washington D.C.'s gossip circuit, that either or both were the "anonymous senior official" who claimed, in a Sept. 5, 2018 Opinion piece in the *New York Times*, to be running a coup against the President on behalf of the "Resistance." The two got roughly equal billing as the probable "Anonymous," with Pence's good friend Dan Coats, the current Director of National Intelligence.

Despite the hideous coup against him motivated by Trump's desire for a decent relationship with Russia, and despite Trump's being fed "Washington Consensus" gruel about how China, rather than London and Wall Street, is the source of American economic misery—nevertheless Trump has, until now, stuck to his guns concerning his desire for positive relations both with Russia and China. Now, Pence has gone for the jugular, so to speak, wildly claiming that China is intervening in the U.S. elections directly, for the purpose of removing Trump from the Presidency. Helga Zepp-La-Rouche has often noted that what the British and the neo-con and neo-liberal American establishment ascribe to the Chinese, is very often nothing but their own aspirations and behavior. It is definitely true in this particular case.

The task of thinking people throughout the world should be to allow the President to see the potential for making the biggest deal of all, the deal for world economic prosperity under a revived New Bretton Woods monetary system, in which money serves the purpose of the physical economic development of the nations of the earth, rather than the imperial needs of empire. As Vladimir Putin has correctly observed, it is foolish for other nations to respond directly to the great internal battle taking place within the United States. Instead, they should be finding and elaborating the flanks which will benefit all human development. Trump really wants to build America anew. He really wants huge new infra-structure projects. He really wants sound bilateral relationships between sovereign nation states. Those concerned about human survival should do everything they can to oblige him.

Vice-Presidents as Rotten Compromises

For an international audience, it is important to put some context around these events in the United States. First regarding the Vice-President and the Vice-Presidency: For most recent American administrations, this post is a compromise involving the pragmatic arrangements necessary to win elections within partisan political parties. Think about Ronald Reagan, who desired to do some really revolutionary things, like Lyndon LaRouche's Strategic Defense Initiative. Reagan made a deal with that rotten Republican faction headed by George H.W. Bush, who pretty much destroyed the potential of the Reagan presidency after the Anglo-Dutch imperialists had the President shot. Reagan did the vice-presidential deal because he needed the Bush electoral machinery to win the election.

Or, take the pairing of Al Gore and Bill Clinton. Gore pretty much sabotaged every genuine Clinton effort directed toward the good of the world, personally sabotaging, for example, face-to-face meetings between President Bill Clinton and Russia's Prime Minister Yevgeny Primakov at a most propitious moment for strategic breakthroughs. As Lyndon LaRouche repeatedly emphasizes, pragmatism is what kills any ability for humankind to truly advance. All such deals involve compromises of fundamental principles, which, more likely than not, will come back to haunt the dealmaker. Such deadly mistakes are typical of partisan politics, and revulsion against them is the reason why a huge sentiment is currently sweeping the United States, seeking the end of both political parties and the birth of a politics based solely on principle.

Donald Trump ran an unprecedented campaign for the Presidency as a Republican—but, in reality, as an independent. Both the Republican and Democratic establishments opposed him with as much ferocity as they could summon. But, as Lyndon LaRouche empha-

William J. Clinton Public Papers

President Bill Clinton (left) with Vice President Al Gore on the South Lawn of the White House, Aug. 10, 1993.

sized when the returns rolled in, the American population, along with other populations internationally, was in revolt against a political establishment which repeatedly sold them out economically and sent them into genocidal wars.

In the U.S., Barack Obama and Hillary Clinton had told them that they had never had it so good; that manufacturing would never come back to the United States; and that their future was in the bread and circuses of a decadent society which had produced massive poverty, an epidemic of addiction killing hundreds every day, and unprecedented suicide rates—while the very rich continued to get, well, very rich. The traditional Republican Party offered the very same poisonous recipes.

Donald Trump promised peace with Russia and China, a return of the U.S. "full-set economy" including a modern infrastructure platform, Glass-Steagall banking separation, what he called the "American system" of political economy, and a return to space exploration. The adherents of the old system in 2016 never really had a chance, despite what the pundits and prognosticators forecast from within their self-satisfied, arrogant fish-bowls.

What Is Mike Pence?

Mike Pence was facing a probable loss in his 2016 re-election effort as Governor of Indiana, and originally endorsed Ted Cruz for President. When Trump destroyed the extant Republican Party bench in the primaries, Pence endorsed Trump and avidly sought the Vice-Presidency. He almost jumped ship when the Billy Bush sexual misconduct tape emerged, flirting with forcing Trump's withdrawal and substituting himself as Presidential candidate. Pence also ran the entire Trump transition, stacking the President's cabinet and significant political appointments with neo-con and establishment allies, like his good friend Dan Coats as Director of National Intelligence. These people not only oppose Donald Trump. They hate him—particularly his determination to end globalism and forge productive relationships with Russia and China, which is an existential threat to the swamp in which they live.

Pence is a Christian Zionist, a very significant power base within the Republican Party, which is crucial to mobilizing the evangelical vote. He also enjoyed ready access to major Republican donors, including those, like Sheldon Adelson, aligned with the Christian Zion-

ists, and David Koch, whose networks played a major role in financing Pence's entire career. Such donors are currently critical to winning a Presidential election in the United States. And, as with all such pragmatic compromises, Trump made it to win the election and to form a government. Although Trump is said to have characterized Pence as the Vice-President from "central casting," he has also reportedly characterized him as slow and "dumb" behind closed doors. Pence's October 4th performance certainly supports that assessment.

Pence gave his speech at the Hudson Institute, which was certainly not an accident. The Hudson Institute was founded by Herman Kahn, the foremost proponent of the insane belief in winnable nuclear war. The Institute has honored Pence with awards. It has gone through several transitions since Kahn and others pro-

CC/ECG tumblr

Sheldon Adelson

pounded their doctrines for killing most of the human race, even moving to Pence's state of Indiana at a certain low point in its financial trajectory.

Following the events of September 11, 2001, it became the Washington, D.C. bastion of the neo-conservatives and Straussians who populated the Bush-Cheney Administration. These are the creeps and overt Satanists who have led the United States into repeated wars in the Middle East under the banner of British Prime Minister Tony Blair's Nazi slogan, "The Responsibility to Protect." Scooter Libby, for example, is Hudson's Senior Vice-President. President Trump has called these adventures, including the wars in Iraq, Libya, and Syria—which murdered hundreds of thousands—the biggest foreign policy mistakes in U.S. history. Hudson receives significant funding from CIA and

Defense Department-related foundations, such as the Bradley Foundation, as well as directly from those agencies themselves. It is also funded by the government of Taiwan.

Pillsbury & Halper: British Right and Left

In his remarks at Hudson, Pence singled out Hudson "scholar" Michael Pillsbury for praise. Pillsbury currently leads the Center for Chinese Strategy at Hudson, a constant font of hatred against everything China has done or is doing. Like Pence, Pillsbury cultivated Trump by aggressively moving to join the Administration soon after the Republican presidential primaries.

Recently, Pillsbury has been regularly appearing on television channels the President watches, such as Fox, to launch acid attacks on the Chinese while claiming that the Chinese respect and honor the President. He says that the Chinese use the Mandarin term for "big brains," or "brainy" to describe Trump. How he knows this is not really explained, but that is true of most of Pillsbury's alleged China scholarship. He tells endless stories on the shakiest of foundations, many of which have served as the basis for billions of dollars in Pentagon expenditures on otherwise very dubious projects. And he has been doing this for a very long time.

Pillsbury claims that he played a starring role in the late 1970s and early 1980s openings to China, earning the notice of then candidate Ronald Reagan by advocating direct military ties with China. An advocate of Kissinger's form of geopolitics and a member of Britain's nefarious International Institute for Strategic Studies, Pillsbury envisioned using extant tensions between the Soviet Union and China at that time, to serve as a major force in destroying the viability of the Soviet bloc.

According to his website, he played a role in providing advanced U.S. defense technologies to China in a bargain that they would pursue the U.S.-assigned use of them against the Soviets, as part of a purported covert plan by the Reagan Administration to collapse the Soviet bloc. These arms sales included new torpedoes, upgrades for jet fighters, and advanced electronics. He also claims to have played a most significant role in providing Stinger missiles to the Afghan Mujahideen. Those groupings, of course, included Osama Bin Laden. Pillsbury also claims that he played a major role

CC/Hudson Institute

Michael Pillsbury (right) with Japanese Prime Minister Shinzo Abe at Hudson Institute headquarters in Washington, D.C.

in founding the National Endowment for Democracy and the United States Institute of Peace, both of which have been the font for U.S. covert regime-change operations throughout the world.

Pillsbury also cultivated a deep friendship with Mohammed Hammoud, the front man for the notorious bank of drugs, terrorism, and money laundering, the Bank of Credit and Commerce International (BCCI), which almost sank his career. According to reports, Pillsbury met with Hammoud on numerous occasions and took funding from him, a situation which landed his boss at the time, Senator Orin Hatch, in an ethics investigation. Not to belabor the point of the rancid Michael Pillsbury being sold to Donald Trump as someone he could trust, it was Robert Mueller, then chief of the Criminal Division of the U.S. Department of Justice, who obstructed and blocked BCCI's final and very much deserved criminal reckoning by the Justice Department.

Following the BCCI fiasco, Pillsbury went to work for Andy Marshall at the Defense Department's Office of Net Assessment, which was spending much of its budget concocting the idea that China represented an unrecognized mortal threat to the United States. Pillsbury joined what was called the "Blue Team" of China hawks, with people who otherwise inhabited the Committee on the Present Danger of Robert Kagan, Paul Wolfowitz and other Neanderthals and Trump-haters, who successively got the United States involved in Iraq and other endless wars in the Middle East—the same wars the President has rightly and righteously condemned.

As reported by Soyoung Ho in the *Washington Monthly* of July 2006, under the title "Panda Slugger: The Dubious Scholarship of Michael Pillsbury, the China Hawk with Rumsfeld's Ear":

> The *Wall Street Journal* took notice of Pillsbury [in 2005] … in a front-page story that described him as "one of the Pentagon's most influential advisers on China, with a direct line to many of Defense Secretary Donald Rumsfeld's top aides." The story observed that China, too, has been "keeping tabs on Mr. Pillsbury." For good reason: Thanks in part to Pillsbury's influence, the Pentagon's 2006 Quadrennial Defense Review, or QDR—the blueprint for future defense strategy and spending—identifies China as the nation with "the greatest potential to compete militarily with the United States." And the Pentagon's most recent annual report to Congress on China's military contains passages that appear to be lifted directly out of Pillsbury's writings, including warnings of "asymmetric programs" in the works. This can get expensive. The *Wall Street Journal* recently reported "the Pentagon now cites China as justification for a range of proposed procurements, most notably a new, multibillion-dollar long-range bomber program.

Ho continued,

> While Pillsbury has achieved prominence within the Defense Secretary's office, many defense experts within the military, government agencies, and universities reject his scholarship as tendentious at best, and their professional distaste is heightened by personal dislike. "Brilliant" and "charming" are words frequently used by acquaintances to describe Pillsbury, but so are "combative," "conspiratorial," and "ruthless."

His career has been one of numerous short-lived jobs, at least three dismissals, and a revoked security clearance.

In Pillsbury's latest book, *The Hundred-Year Marathon*, he claims that the Chinese, above all, are masters of deception and that Chinese military strategy is drawn from its Warring States Period, a period of disunified strife more than 2,200 years ago. He says that, unlike most Western analysts, he has cultivated relations with nationalist factions in the Peoples' Liberation Army who have provided him with unique access to their views and strategies.

He claims that these masters of deception have told him, a recognized China-hater of some years standing, their secret plan for becoming the world hegemon by the year 2049, the one hundredth anniversary of the Chinese Revolution. He claims that Xi Jinping is covertly such a nationalist and deceiver. The reason he says the Chinese bequeathed their master plan upon him was to use him to enhance their status in China. As they say in the game of outright scams, if you believe that, I have a bridge I can sell you.

The other side of the China bashing inherited by this President, is the neo-liberal version. As opposed to Pillsbury, who leads the neo-con tribe, the neo-liberals have been led by one Stefan Halper. Halper's Defense Department and British intelligence work includes a book, *The Beijing Consensus: Legitimizing Authoritarianism in Our Time*. It is to be noted that when he was not laying out how to geopolitically isolate and contain China, Halper worked for the British and the CIA to entrap volunteers for the Trump presidential campaign on British soil, thus fabricating the leads which led to the unprecedented FBI counterintelligence investigation of Donald Trump's campaign and the illegal Robert Mueller investigation of the Trump Administration.

The Pence Speech

In his speech, Pence gives vast lip service to Donald Trump's friendship with Xi Jinping and the long history of U.S./China friendship, while attempting to escalate

Stefan Halper

the present trade dispute between the two countries into exactly the type of geopolitical confrontation the President condemns. The President has stated emphatically that the United States is not going to tell other nations how to live. Yet, Pence takes up exactly and extensively, the hypocritical human rights and democracy-promotion themes endlessly spun as the pillars of U.S. regime change operations. In the run-up to this speech, Pence and Congressional allies arranged arms sales to Taiwan, also inflaming that very sensitive issue.

The second major theme struck by Pence is the trade dispute between the U.S. and China. There is no question but that U.S. companies exported many U.S. jobs to China and Asia, seeking the cheapest source of labor under the inhuman regime called "globalism" and "free trade." Under the plan for the world economy crafted by the British and their U.S. satraps in the Trilateral Commission and the Council on Foreign Relations in the early 1980s, their export of U.S. jobs and major strategic parts of the U.S. economy was part of a plan for "controlled disintegration" of the advanced sector economies.

The United States was to become a post-industrial service and consumer economy, while China and other nations were to be brought up to the fixed rates of production once enjoyed by the United States, but no further. In effect, the extant supply-chain of the world's economy was outsourced throughout the world, to wherever the price of labor was the cheapest.

What this conspiracy of idiots failed to recognize is that any fixed mode of production or technology will ultimately fail and collapse because it disobeys the fundamental physical laws of the universe. Successful economies must enjoy high rates of technological progress and fundamental scientific breakthroughs to be sustainable over a period of generations. Otherwise they die through technological attrition.

Thus, while Pence, Pillsbury, Peter Navarro, Steve Bannon, and other dim-witted fools paint China as a ruthless pirate that stole America's future and continues to do so, the reality is that the City of London and Wall Street, and their free trade and post-industrial madness, are the actual culprits. Further, continued adherence to the present monetarist regimes of Wall Street and the City of London and their globalist prescriptions is about to make the situation even worse, as the bloated debt bubble accumulated since the 2008 collapse teeters on the edge of explosion. And that presents the danger of bringing every nation down.

As Hermann Kahn's fellows at the Rand Corporation meticulously proved, Hitler's war machine failed because it expanded its economy only laterally and cannibalized its labor force in a genocide. In this trade dispute, some, in both China and the United States, seem to view computer technologies, artificial intelligence, biotechnology, and robotics as the crown jewels of the realm. But these prized, allegedly future technologies are only linear and lateral extensions of existing technologies and known scientific principles. They have existed in the bill of materials of the United States for some years and have utterly failed to produce significant advances in productivity.

World Needs Sovereign, 'Full-Set' Economies

The urgent question posed in the U.S./China trade dispute is how "full set economies" can be built in both countries such that they are self-sufficient and can reproduce their populations at the highest levels of development, as specified by Lyndon LaRouche. What does it matter if the United States gets more of the worldwide supply chain back, if it is based on an old mode of production and does not result in the fundamental advances in productivity necessary to actually jumpstart the economy?

Fusion energy, space exploration, basic science at the very frontiers of human knowledge, together with massive new city-building and infrastructure, are what is required in both countries to prevent catastrophe as the speculative worldwide bubble economy collapses. And the basis for rapidly doing this across the world can

Artist's conception of China's space lab Tiangong-1 (left) shown docking with the Shenzhou-8 spacecraft.

China's EAST, or Experimental and Advanced Superconducting Tokamak fusion reactor.

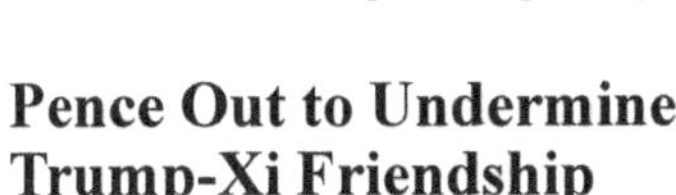
Xinhua

Xinhua

only be found in a fixed exchange-rate world monetary system issuing long-term, low-interest credit for development, whose creation has now become an urgent issue of human survival.

As with Lyndon LaRouche's and Ronald Reagan's Strategic Defense Initiative, the United States and China should be collaborating jointly now on crash programs for breakthroughs in these advanced areas, which are now crucial for the long-term economic survival of both countries and the human race as a whole. It is extremely important now to remember that this was the Reagan offer to the Soviets—joint development for the good of humanity. It is that prospect which Pence, Pillsbury, and their British imperial friends are mobilized against. It is that prospect which Donald Trump could bring into being, but which his opponents are determined to prevent, at all costs. The joint approaches to settling the nuclear and other issues of the Korean peninsula are an initial step in that direction.

In his dumb speech, Pence made a variety of claims about China's alleged geopolitical aggressiveness in the Western Pacific and made allusions to encircling China with an alliance involving the United States, Japan, South Korea, and India. He did this without regard for the very delicate negotiations being conducted simulta-

neously by Secretary of State Mike Pompeo in North Korea, indicating that Pence's faction is intent on blowing up that prospect for peace. The pipe dream about a U.S.-Japan-South Korea-India alliance is exactly that. Aside from the strategically blind United States, the other putative members of this alliance fully realize the actual potential and meaning of China's great One Belt, One Road Initiative, and want to fully participate.

With respect to Pence's claims about alleged Chinese aggressiveness and imperial aims in the Western Pacific, one wag commented that the claim amounts to demanding that China apologize for its geographic location in the midst of a deliberate encirclement by American bases, which is the reality of Barack Obama's "Asia pivot" policy.

Pence Out to Undermine Trump-Xi Friendship

But, by far, the vilest part of Pence's performance was aimed squarely at undermining the personal relationship between Xi and Trump. In that respect, Pence claimed that China is now in a "whole nation" mobilization to remove Donald Trump as President because of the trade dispute between the two nations. He cited the fact that China ill-advisedly placed ads in Iowa newspapers condemning the President's tariffs. This reactive gaffe clearly failed to understand the present U.S. political environment, and is the sole factual basis for all of Mike Pence's bellicose and false claims about Chinese election interference aimed at Trump.

The rest of it is based on alleged classified intelligence reports which are almost certainly as bogus as those produced by the cherry-picked intelligence analysts who claimed massive Russian interference in the U.S. elections to elect Trump. After all, Pence's good friend, Director of National Intelligence Dan Coats, has not balked at public rebukes of President Trump concerning Trump's continued belief in Putin's good faith—and he most certainly wouldn't balk at fabricating evidence and cooking the books to destroy Trump's relationship to Xi Jinping.

FIRST PUBLISHED IN *EIR*, NOVEMBER 3, 1995

Riemann Refutes Euler: Behind an Earthshaking Scientific Discovery

by Lyndon H. LaRouche, Jr.

Editors' note: *The magazine **21st Century Science & Technology** published, in its Winter 1995 edition, an English translation of a collection of early writings of Bernhard Riemann. We publish here Lyndon La-Rouche's introduction, "Riemann Refutes Euler," by permission of **21st Century**.*

In the following pages, **21st Century** presents the first known publication in English translation, of a group of posthumously published early writings of the famous physicist Bernhard Riemann (1826-1866).[1] These have the special significance of providing some relatively indispensable background for understanding how Riemann came to develop his earthshaking discoveries of 1853-1854.[2]

The special relevance of these pieces, pertains to the fact, that there can be no competent appraisal of Riemann's work, which does not treat his writings as, like those of Karl Weierstrass, a devastating refutation

of Leonhard Euler's savage attacks on Gottfried Leibniz.[3] The formal issue is the question, cloaked in a discussion of mathematical series, whether or not mathematical discontinuities exist.[4] The relevant substantive issue behind these attacks on Leibniz by the Eighteenth-Century newtonians, Dr. Samuel Clarke and Leonhard Euler, is, much more today than during Riemann's time,

---

1. See **Bernhard Riemann's Gesammelte Mathematische Werke**, Heinrich Weber, ed. (New York: Dover Publications reprint, 1953), *"Fragmente philosophischen Inhalts,"* pp. 507-538. A more recent reprint of the same, Heinrich Weber's second edition (Stuttgart: B.G. Teubner, 1902), is Vaduz, Liechtenstein: Saendig Reprint Verlag Hans R. Wohlwend. Hereinafter, this is identified as **Riemann Werke**.

2. See Bernhard Riemann, *"Über die Hypothesen, welche der Geometrie zu Grunde liegen"* ("On the Hypotheses Which Underlie Geometry"), **Riemann Werke**, pp. 272-287. This is the famous June 10, 1854 habilitation dissertation, to which Albert Einstein referred, in identifying Riemann's work as a root of General Relativity. On the dating of the work embodied in this dissertation, 1853-1854, see H. Weber's reference to Riemann's note, which dates the discovery underlying the paper to "March 1, 1853": **Werke**, p. 508.

3. On Euler's attack on Leibniz, see Lyndon H. LaRouche, Jr., **The Science of Christian Economy** (Washington: Schiller Institute, 1991), Appendix XI, "Euler's Fallacies on the Subjects of Infinite Divisibility and Leibniz's Monads," pp. 407-425. That appendix includes the sections of Euler's **Letters to a German Princess** (dated by him May 5, 1761) in which his second explicit attack on Leibniz is made. The first occurred as his role in the scandalous case of Pierre-Louis Maupertuis, whose exposed fraud on the subject of "least action" led to Maupertuis's 1753 ouster from direction of the Berlin Academy; Euler was the principal accomplice of Maupertuis in perpetrating that hoax. We emphasize the primary coincidence between Riemann and Weierstrass here, not their secondary differences in approach.

4. See Leibniz-Clarke correspondence on the subject of the relationship between infinite series and the differential calculus. (G.W. Leibniz, **Philosophical Papers and Letters,** edited by Leroy E. Loemker, 2nd edition [Dordrecht: D. Reidel, 1969, reprinted Boston: Kluwer Academic, 1989], pp. 675-721.) Although Leibniz's development of the differential calculus had roots in some of his earlier activities, the archival evidence is, that what became known as Leibniz's calculus was actually developed during 1672-1676, in Paris, at Jean-Baptiste Colbert's Royal Academy of Science. Leibniz's first paper, presenting the discovery, was submitted for publication, in Paris, in 1676, immediately prior to his return to Germany. Isaac Newton's international reputation, and the Newton-Clarke attack on Leibniz, was created by Venice's Paris-based Abbot Antonio Conti (1677-1749), who sponsored a network of salons throughout Europe, a network devoted to the principal mission of seeking to discredit Leibniz, and build up Newton's reputation. Dr. Samuel Clarke was an agent of Conti, as were the Berlin circles of Maupertuis and Euler.

Bernhard Riemann (above) and Leonhard Euler (right). "Like Leibniz before him, Riemann's discovery demonstrates that formal mathematical-physics schemes do not embody the potentiality of a truth-doctrine. To find truth, we must depart the domain of mathematics, and go over into another domain, the realm of experimental physics."

whether physics is a branch of mathematics, or mathematics a branch of physics.

As in the concluding sentence of his famous 1854 habilitation dissertation, Riemann demonstrated that, to settle the underlying issues of mathematics, one must depart that domain, into physics.[5] That statement plants Riemann, like his sponsor Karl Gauss before him, fully within the domain of physics, rather than the virtual reality which one associates with the influence of Bertrand Russell and the Bourbaki *Golem* upon much of today's teaching of mathematics. The posthumously published papers presented in English translation here, bear directly on Riemann's development of his approach to that issue.

Riemann and Economics

21st Century's attention to Riemann reflects my own original work in a branch of physical science founded by Leibniz, known as physical economy. My discoveries in this field supplied the principal impetus for the mid-1970s founding of the Fusion Energy Foundation, which ricocheted into the later founding of **21st Century** magazine. Although the principal part of my discoveries were not prompted by Riemann's work, the approach adopted for solving the mathematical problems posed by those discoveries was prompted almost entirely by Riemann's habilitation dissertation, leading to the designation of "LaRouche-Riemann Method."[6]

To introduce Riemann's posthumously published papers, I indicate the features of his dissertation which are most relevant to the problems of physical economy. To that end, consider, first, the place which mathematical discontinuities occupy in Riemann's discovery, and then, the significance of Riemann's emphasis on what he terms *Geistesmassen* in the posthumously published papers.

---

5. "*Es führt dies hinüber in das Gebiet einer andern Wissenschaft, in das Gebiet der Physik, welches wohl die Natur der heutigen Veranlassung nicht zu betreten erlaubt.*" ("This leads into the domain of another science, the realm of physics, which the nature of today's occasion does not permit us to enter.") Habilitation dissertation, **Riemann Werke**, p. 286.

6. See Lyndon H. LaRouche, Jr., "Why Most Nobel Prize Economists Are Quacks," *Executive Intelligence Review,* July 28, 1995, and Lyndon H. LaRouche, Jr., "Non-Newtonian Mathematics for Economists," **Executive Intelligence Review**, Aug. 11, 1995.

First, to define the significance of mathematical discontinuities, I restate Riemann's point of departure in his dissertation in my own words.

The origin of modern mathematics lies in what is commonly identified as a "Euclidean" notion of simple space-time. This idea of space-time pretends to represent the real universe, which it does not represent. It is an idea which is not a creation of the senses, but, rather, of the naive imagination. We merely imagine that space is defined by three senses of direction (backward-forward, up-down, side-to-side), and imagine that these might be extended without limit, and in perfectly uninterrupted continuity. We imagine that time is a single, limitless dimension of perfect continuity: backward-forward. Taken together, these presumptions of the imagination define a four-dimensional space-time manifold, or, in other words, a quadruply-extended space-time manifold.

The naive imagination attempts to locate perceptible bodies and their motions within such a quadruply extended manifold. It may be said fairly, that our imaginary space-time manifold is used as a kind of mental mirror, upon which we attempt to project reflections of motion of bodies in space-time. The result of such projections is a simple "Euclidean" sort of algebraic mathematics, which, we soon discover, is not a mathematics of the real universe.

Classical experiments, typified by the measurement of the curvature of the Earth's surface by the ancient Eratosthenes of Plato's Academy at Athens,[7] supply measurable demonstration that the motion of bodies in physical space-time does not correspond to what a naive, algebraic notion of space-time suggests. We must add non-space-time "dimensions," such as the notions of "mass," "charge," and so forth, to derive a mathematics which agrees with our measurement of the motions which are reflected, from physical space-time, upon that imaginary mirror known as simple space-time.[8]

Thus, in place of a four-dimensional space-time of the imagination, the attempt to explore physical space-time presents us with a physical-space-time manifold of many more dimensions than the four dimensions of naive space-time. We call these added factors "dimensions," because they can be scaled, according to the ordering-principle of "greater than" and "less than," as we do the dimensions of naive space-time. Instead of saying $n+4$ dimensions, we include the four in our count of $n;$ we speak, thus, of a "physical-space-time manifold of n dimensions." Then, commonly, we attempt to portray motion within that physical-space-time, of n dimensions, in terms of its imaginary reflection upon a four-fold space-time.

In each case, the addition of a validatable new "dimension" to the physical-space-time manifold of reference, corresponds to a change in measurement, a change in the yardstick we must employ to measure the relevant motion, or analogous form of action. For example, Eratosthenes estimated that the Earth was a spheroid of about 7850 miles, from pole to pole (not a bad estimate for the time).[9] This meant, that to measure motion along the surface of the Earth, we must use a yardstick of spherical trigonometry, rather than one appropriate to a simple Euclidean plane. Similarly, once Ole Rømer had demonstrated, in 1676, that the radiation of light was governed by a principle of retarded potential, Christiaan Huygens, in 1677, generalized principles of reflection and refraction accordingly,[10] and, Jean Bernoulli and Leibniz demonstrated that the mathematics of the transcendental domain's special relativity must supersede the algebraic methods of Galileo, Descartes, and Newton.[11]

The validation of the necessary addition of such an added physical dimension, by measurement, implies the challenge to be considered here. Each such addition signifies, that instead of an n-fold physical-space-time manifold, n is superseded by $(n+1)$. This gives us a generalized term of topology, which we might express symbolically by $(n+1)/n$. The series of changes, from n to $n+1$ dimensions, is associated with a series of changes in the choice of the yardstick which we must employ to measure the relevant physical action.[12]

---

7. See "How Eratosthenes Measured the Unseen" (Figure 2), in Lyndon H. LaRouche, Jr., "Kenneth Arrow Runs Out of Ideas, But Not Words," **21st Century,** Fall 1995, pp. 34-53.

8. This image is an accurate representation of the intent of Plato's reference to shadows which reality casts upon the imagination, as if these shadows were reflections on the wall of a cave's firelit interior.

9. **Greek Mathematical Works**, Ivor Thomas, trans., 2 vols. (Cambridge, Mass.: Harvard University Press, 1980), Vol. II, p. 273, note c.

10. Christiaan Huygens, **A Treatise on Light** (New York: Dover Publications reprint, 1962).

11. The "brachystochrone problem": Jean Bernoulli (1696). The equivalence of least time to least action.

12. This does not justify the presumptions of some popularized notions of a differential geometry. The basis for that word of warning will be made clearer below.

This is also the problem which confronts us, in physical economy, as one may attempt to define the correspondence between scientific and technological progress, on the one side, and, on the other side, a general, resulting increase in the productive powers of labor, per capita, per household, and per square kilometer. For that case, the type of yardstick used is termed *potential relative population-density*; that yardstick changes its scale (per capita, per square kilometer) as the level of applied scientific and technological progress advances.

Science and Metaphor

All of the issues posed by Riemann's habilitation dissertation, while most profound, are so elementary that they might be understood at the level of a good secondary school's graduate. Once we accept his intention in that location, that paper is among the most lucid pieces of prose ever supplied to the literature of fundamental scientific discoveries. Admittedly, most of the classroom's putatively authoritative commentators have conveyed a contrary, confused view of this work. The failure of all such commentaries examined, is that the commentators, by refusing to accept the fact of what Riemann is saying, project upon him an intention which is axiomatically contrary to his own.

The axiomatic failures of such authoritative commentators occur on two levels.

Closer to the surface, they have sought to defend such post-1815 authorities in taught mathematics as Newton, Euler, Augustin Cauchy, et al. from the devastating refutation provided by Riemann's discovery. This centers around Euler's argument against Leibniz. That relatively more superficial axiomatic assertion, is the hysterical insistence of the positivists, that, ultimately, mathematical discontinuities do not exist.[13]

On the deeper level, there is a more devastating issue, which the opponents of Leibniz and Riemann refuse to debate.

The radical positivists of the Bourbaki cult exemplify this deeper issue. The peculiar, Ockhamite deism of such positivist ideologues, is the dogma, that all questions of science must be settled by mathematical proofs delivered upon a blackboard, or, by a modern digital-computer system. Every demonstration that mathematical formalism is not the god of science, whether by Plato and his academy after him, or from moderns such as Leibniz or Riemann, fills such positivists with an obscene, irrationalist rage, akin in spirit and rationality to that of Marat's or Danton's Jacobin mob.

This deeper of the two levels of axiomatic issues, underlies the assignment of Abbot Antonio Conti's agent, Dr. Samuel Clarke, for the attacks upon Leibniz. This is the issue underlying the savage, posthumous attacks upon Leibniz by the Conti salon's Euler. This was also the basis for the hyena-like attack, led by the devotees of Ernst Mach, upon Max Planck, during the period of World War I.[14]

Once we acknowledge the primary historical fact of mathematical-physical knowledge, that each of those discoveries of physical principle which is validated by the appropriate measurement, presents mathematics with a topological challenge of the indicated $(n+1)/n$ form, mathematical formalism is stripped of that attributed, god-like authority which the devotees of Euler and the Bourbaki cult defend so fanatically.[15] Like Leibniz before him, Riemann's discovery demonstrates that formal mathematical-physics schemes do not embody the potentiality of a truth-doctrine. To find truth, we must depart the domain of mathematics, and go over into another domain, the realm of experimental physics.

The key to all among these, and derived formal issues of mathematical physics, is the connection between the erroneous insistence, that, ultimately, no discontinuities exist in mathematics, and the deeper assumption (also false), as among the followers of the Bourbaki dogma, that mathematics can be a truth-doctrine.

It is admissible to state, that any consistent mathematical physics of a specific, n-fold physical-space-time manifold, can be read as if it were a formal, deductive theorem-lattice. In this interpretation, it appears that every theorem of that lattice has the qualifying at-

---

13. Formally, Euler's assertion was a defense of the purely arbitrary assumption of the naive Euclidean imagination, that linear extension is perfectly continuous without limit. Since Euler's supposed proof of that assertion depends absolutely upon the assertion of that axiom which it purports to prove, Euler's famous tautology proves nothing at all. Euler's folly on this point is the hereditary origin, via Lagrange and Laplace, of Cauchy's bowdlerization of Gottfried Leibniz's version of a calculus.

14. That attack upon Planck, first from within the German-speaking scientific community of the World War I interval, was continued in the savagery of Niels Bohr and other accomplices of Bertrand Russell, during the period of the famous 1920s Solvay Conference sessions.

15. This is literally an ancient issue. This topological challenge is the same ontological paradox, of the "One" and "Many," posed by Plato's *Parmenides*.

tribute of being a proposition which has been shown to be not-inconsistent with whatever set of axioms and postulates underlie that lattice in its entirety.[16] Such a set of axioms and postulates is identified by both Plato and Riemann as an *hypothesis*, in contrast to the illiterate's misuse of the same term in Newton's famous "*et hypotheses non fingo.*"[17]

The literate usage of "hypothesis," is mandatory in reading even the title of Riemann's June 1854 dissertation, even before proceeding to the body of the text. The key to a literate reading of Riemann's dissertation, is that a topological transformation typified by the transition from a mathematically *n*-fold physical-space-time manifold, to a manifold of (n+1) dimensions, is a transformation in the set of axioms and postulates underlying mathematical physics.

Consequently, the history of those discoveries of physical principle which, like Eratosthenes' discovery of an estimated curvature of the Earth, are validated by the relevant measurement, presents us with a succession of topological changes within mathematical physics, a series of changes which has the form of the "One"/"Many" paradox of Plato's **Parmenides.** In this instance, the "Many" are represented by a series of hypotheses; the challenge is to discover a higher principle, an *higher hypothesis*, a "One," which defines a generative principle by means of which the series of hypotheses, the "Many," is ordered "transfinitely." If Riemann's dissertation is read in any different sense than this platonic one, the resulting commentary upon the text is a scientifically illiterate one, no matter what the putative classroom authority of the commentator.

Riemann adopts a view of mathematical physics based upon the succession of advances in those discoveries of physical principle which have been validated crucially by relevant measurement, such as Eratosthenes' estimate for curvature of the Earth typifies that principle of measurement. Riemann's view of this topological transformation underlying mathematical physics' progress, thus defines progress in mathematical physics in terms of a sequence of absolute mathematical discontinuities within a formalist reading of mathematical physics itself. It defines Newton, Euler, and Cauchy, for example, as victims of their own scientific illiteracy, victims of an ontological paradox, of the "One"/"Many" form, which they could neither solve, nor comprehend—and, apparently, did not wish to comprehend.

In each case, one formal theorem-lattice is distinguished from another by any change in the axiomatic content, from that of the hypothesis underlying one, to that of the hypothesis underlying the other; every theorem of the second lattice is formally inconsistent with any theorem of the first. The difference between the two hypotheses, is a true, and relatively absolute mathematical discontinuity. Such a "discontinuity" has the same significance in mathematical physics as the proper understanding of the term "metaphor" in Classical forms of poetry or drama. What "discontinuity" signifies respecting the formalities of a consistent mathematical physics, is precisely what "metaphor" signifies for a Classical poem or drama.[18] The understanding of this relationship between metaphor and mathematical discontinuity, is the key to the first of the posthumously published documents, "On Psychology & Metaphysics," presented in the following pages.

In physics, a mathematical discontinuity appears as a mere mark. The magnitude of this mark is of *transinfinitesimal* smallness, so small that no calculable arithmetic magnitude can measure it, yet it exists, nonetheless, as a phenomenon: apparently as a mark of separation of all magnitudes which are less, from all magnitudes which are greater.[19] This mark signifies the functional presence, outside the realm of mathematical formalities, of the mathematical-physical form of what we recognize in Classical poetry as a metaphor.

---

16. E.g.: What Euler defends, by means of a rather silly tautology, in his 1761 attack upon Leibniz, is the naive, Euclidean, axiomatic assumption of the perfect persistence of linearization indefinitely, into the very large and very small.

17. **Riemann Werke**, p. 525: "*Das Wort Hypothese hat jetzt eine etwas andere Bedeutung als bei Newton. Man pflegt jetzt unter Hypothese Alles zu Erscheinungen Hinzugedachte zu verstehen.*"

18. The relevant problem is that, many miseducated readers with advanced degrees in arts have the same difficulty in coping with the term "metaphor," which radical positivists experience with the term "mathematical discontinuity." Beginning the early Seventeenth Century, the empiricists, such as Thomas Hobbes, launched a vile, energetic, and persisting campaign to eradicate the use of metaphor and the subjunctive mood from English-language usage. The recent emergence of that radical-existentialist decadence known as the "deconstructionism" of Professor Jacques Derrida, et al., is the outgrowth of a centuries-long campaign by the empiricists and logical positivists, and related linguistics specialists, to locate the origin of written language, even Classical poetry, in "text" as such, rather than the irony-rich domain of speech.

19. In the extremely small, discontinuities are compared in respect to their mathematical cardinality, not as arithmetic values. Hence, with deference to Georg Cantor, this distinction is designated here by the usage of "transinfinitesimally small."

Riemann's 'Geistesmassen'

The fact that all true metaphors are singularities, is the key to an accurate understanding of Riemann's use of *Geistesmassen*, translated here as "thought masses," in the first of the posthumously published papers, "On Psychology and Metaphysics." As an illustration of the principle involved, consider the case of metaphor in either a Classical form of strophic poem, or a song-setting of such a poem by a Mozart,[20] Beethoven, Schubert, Schumann, or Brahms.[21] This case, of the Classical strophic poem, and its musical setting according to principles of motivic thorough-composition, is key for understanding the mental processes by means of which a validatable discovery of new scientific principle is generated.[22] This is also an example of the conception posed by Plato's treatment of the "One/Many" ontological paradox in his **Parmenides** and other late dialogues.[23]

In the successful Classical poem, efficiently illustrated as to form by Goethe's simple **Mailied**,[24] the strophes represent a succession of metaphors, which march, one after the other, toward a conclusion. The metaphorical attribution of each of those strophes is generated by ironies, to such effect that no proper attribution of either a confining literal or a symbolic meaning for that strophe is to be permitted. The concluding metaphor, especially its final couplet, changes radically the metaphorical attribution—e.g., the "meaning"—of the poem as a whole. It is that concluding, subsuming metaphor, which identifies the idea of the poem taken in its entirety.

The literate reading of such a poem, or its Classical song-setting, demands a repeated review of the completed poem, until the point is reached that two conditions are satisfied: first, that the idea of the completed poem as a whole is clear; second, that the relationship of each step of progress within the poem, to the reaching of the conclusion, is clear.[25] The satisfaction of that requirement establishes the idea of the poem as a whole, in the mind, as the product of a tension between two, literally platonic qualities of idea. The first, is the idea of the completed poem in its entirety; this idea remains unchanged, from prior to the re-reading of the first line, to the momentary silence following the reading of the last line. The second idea, is the successive metamorphoses which the idea of the poem undergoes, in proceeding from the beginning to the end. In Plato, that latter quality of idea is identified as the *Becoming*. It is the tension between the fixed conception, the idea of the completed poem as a whole, and the metamorphical character of the process of Becoming, by which the perfected idea is reached, which is the "energy" of the poem.

The same requirement applies to the performance of any Classical musical composition. In the simplest case of such a musical performance, it is the performer's memory of reaching the perfected (completed) composition, which creates the tension of reenacting the performance of the metamorphosis, the tension between the perfected idea of the composition, and the moment of development in mid-performance.

The singularity in question is generated by the difference in direction of time-sense—backwards versus forwards—of the two, interacting ideas respecting the poem or musical composition in mid-performance.

The same principle characterizes Eratosthenes' estimate of the curvature of the Earth's surface: the principle of development uncovered, by re-experiencing the mutually contradictory individual readings of the midday sundials, to locate a generating principle of change which is consistent with the final result. For Eratosthenes, the key to the generating principle becomes the relationship between the perimeter of a circle and a pencil of lines, from a momentarily fixed position of the point corresponding to the Sun, to the Earth. Thus, Eratosthenes gave a reasonable estimation of the Earth's curvature, approximately twenty-two centuries before

---

20. After Mozart's first song composed in the new mode of motivic thorough-composition, his setting of Johann Goethe's "Das Veilchen" ("The Violet"). See **A Manual on the Rudiments of Tuning and Registration**, John Sigerson and Kathy Wolfe, eds. (Washington: Schiller Institute, 1992), Chapter 11, pp. 199-228.

21. Op. cit., pp. 220-221. Note the reference to Gustav Jenner, **Johannes Brahms als Mensch, Lehrer und Künstler: Studien und Erlebnisse** (Marburg an der Lahn: N.G. Elwert'sche Verlagsbuchhandlung, 1930). Jenner's account of Brahms' instruction to him on composing a song for a strophic poem, is directly relevant to the point being developed at this point in the text, above.

22. See Lyndon H. LaRouche, Jr., "Musical Memory and Thorough-Composition," *Executive Intelligence Review*, Sept. 1, 1995, pp. 50-63.

23. Plato's *Parmenides* is to be considered as a kind of prefatory piece for all of his later dialogues. In it, he poses the challenge, the ontological paradox, which is the subject addressed in its various aspects by all of the other late dialogues.

24. LaRouche, "Musical Memory and Thorough-Composition," p. 55. See note 22.

25. See Jenner's account of his instructions from Brahms, on memorizing a poem with sufficient thoroughness to satisfy those requirements, before undertaking to provide a song-setting for it. See note 21.

any person saw that curvature.

These examples, from poetry, music, and the work of Plato's Academy of Athens, are each and all examples of *platonic ideas*, the quality of ideas to which Riemann assigns the term *Geistesmassen*. In physical science generally, such ideas have initially the apparent character of ideas arising from vicious inconsistencies within observations made by aid of sense-perception, inconsistencies which mock both naive sense-certainty and generally accepted scientific opinion. Relatively often, that mockery occurs in the most cruelly devastating way. Those ideas which purport to identify the generating principle responsible for this paradox, and which are validated by relevant modes of measurement, represent valid discoveries of physical principle. Those qualities of proven principle are classically identified as *platonic ideas*. Each and all of the validated ideas of "dimensionality" in an *n*-fold physical-space-time manifold, have this quality of platonic idea.

Thus, all such ideas have the form of paradoxical singularities relative to the pre-existing mathematical domain of reference. The character of these ideas as singularities arises from the way in which their existence is generated *subjectively*: by the same kind of processes underlying the reading and composition of a valid Classical strophic poem. The quality of "singularity," and the associated form of mathematical discontinuity, arises from the opposing senses of time associated with the interplay of perfected ideas with the process of their development.[26]

These metaphors can never be deduced from the mathematics, or other form of language employed. Within the language itself, they appear merely in the reflected form of singularities, such as either mathematical discontinuities or other paradoxical adumbrations reflected into the language-medium. The ontological existence of the singularity lies outside the form of generation of the relevant mark within the domain of the language itself.

Thus, every theorem which claims to deny the existence of discontinuities within mathematics, such as Euler's, is based upon *the tautological fallacy of composition, of using constructions premised axiomatically on linearization, to prove the utterly irrelevant point, that any construction of this type is incapable of acknowledging any mathematical existence which is not linear!*

The relevant formal mathematical discontinuity, or literary paradox, is merely the mark which the metaphor imposes, as its footprint, upon the formally defined medium of language. The actual metaphor, which the adumbrated mark, or paradox reflects, exists only outside the medium. It lies within three locations. It lies, first, in the substance of the process which the language is attempting to describe. It also lies, secondly, in the mental processes of the scientist, or the artist. It exists, thirdly, within the sovreign mental processes of those members of the audience who have responded Socratically to the mark of the singularity, by generating in their own mind a replication of the idea which has imposed its mark upon the medium of communication.

In mathematical physics, the validation of the ideas corresponding to such marks occurs commonly through measurements which demonstrate, that those ideas correspond efficiently to an effect which is not in correspondence with the old ideas which the new ideas profess to supersede.

There is a most notable illustration of this point in the case of Riemann's paper, published in 1860, "On the Propagation of Plane Air Waves of Finite Amplitude."[27] The fact that acceleration toward speeds above the speed of sound generates a singularity, was recognized by Riemann as showing the existence of the transsonic phenomena studied by such followers as Ludwig Prandtl and Adolf Busemann. It was this principle of Riemann's which resulted, through the mediation of a German aerospace specialist, in the first successful powered, post-World War II, supersonic flight by a U.S. aircraft. This was in contrast to the failed contrary opinion expressed by such frequent adversaries of Riemann's work as Hermann Helmholtz, Lord Rayleigh, and Theodor von Karman.[28]

---

26. The proper notions of topology are derived from this consideration.

27. *"Über die Fortpflanzung ebener Luftwellen von endlicher Schwingungsweite,"* **Riemann Werke**, pp. 156-175. This was published in an English translation by Uwe Henke and Steven Bardwell, in the Fusion Energy Foundation's *International Journal of Fusion Energy*, Vol. 2, No. 3, 1980, pp. 1-23.

28. There is a relevant story behind the Fusion Energy Foundation's publication of that translation. During the middle to late 1970s, the Fusion Energy Foundation (FEF) gained an international reputation for its important work in promoting inertial confinement fusion. As a consequence of this, in 1978, two representatives of the FEF, Mr. Charles B. Stevens, Jr., and Dr. Steven Bardwell, were invited to the Soviet Union to participate in an international scientific conference on inertial confinement. Prior to their departure, these two FEF representatives met with LaRouche and others, at a Bronx location, to obtain LaRouche's list of requirements for that Moscow visit. LaRouche requested that they ask Soviet scientists for unclassified documents pertaining to the

In the relatively more obvious type of case, such as the cited Eratosthenes case, the empirical validation of such a singularity is accomplished by measurements which lie within the domain of arithmetic magnitudes. However, this is not the only primary form of empirical proof of a platonic idea. As Riemann's referenced paper on shock-waves illustrates the point, in some cases, it is the existence of a non-arithmetic singularity, which has precise cardinality, but not arithmetic magnitude, which presents us the mathematical form of the required proof. Riemann's success in forecasting a class of phenomena not necessarily limited to this cited case, not only powered transsonic/supersonic flight, but isentropic compression in thermonuclear ignition, is an example of this.

Leibniz's Universal Characteristic

Respecting the ontological implications of metaphor itself, within these posthumously published pieces, Riemann picks up on a theme addressed earlier by Leibniz, and later revived by the present writer. We must consider the fact, that those efficient platonic ideas recognizable as validated discoveries of principle, are generated as discoveries within those sovreign mental processes of the individual which are impenetrable by symbolic communications-media, such as a formal mathematics. Yet, despite the ethereal quality one might be tempted to attribute wrongly to such mental processes, the result of such ideas is an increase of the human species' physical power to command nature in general.

In this respect, these papers of Riemann turn our attention back to Leibniz's notion of a *Universal Characteristic*, which subsumes, commonly, non-living, living, and cognitive processes within our universe. This is the topical area addressed in the first two of the posthumously published papers: "I. On Psychology and Metaphysics," and "II. Epistemological issues." After the writing of these papers, Riemann's published work does not refer explicitly again to such epistemological

underpinnings of science. From 1854 on, his published work limits itself essentially to mathematical physics, with some impingement upon biophysics,[29] although he clearly did not abandon that personal standpoint in his thinking about mathematical-physics matters. Therein lies some of the special importance of the posthumously published papers for identifying the deeper implications of Riemann's work as a whole.

My own discoveries in physical-economy were rooted in my youthful profession as a follower of Leibniz, and in my developing a rigorous defense of Leibniz against Immanuel Kant's attacks upon him, the latter a matter which bears directly upon the issue of Leibniz's notion of a Universal Characteristic. Furthermore, my discoveries were provoked by both the positivist excesses of Norbert Wiener's "information theory" and the similar incompetence of the work in systems analysis by one of Wiener's followers, John von Neumann; these positivist concoctions I had treated as parodies of Kant's attack on Leibniz. For this reason, my rereading of Riemann brought to that reading the same emphasis upon Leibniz's Universal Characteristic which we encounter in the first two items among Riemann's posthumously published pieces.

The kernel of Wiener's hoax in "information theory," was to adopt and misuse a term, "negative entropy," which had been used earlier chiefly to identify the qualitative distinction between living and non-living processes as they present themselves on the scale of macrophysics.[30]

In successful modern physical economies, my field of study, the biological appearance of "negative entropy" is echoed by the requirement that the ratio of relative "free energy" to "energy of the system" must not decrease, despite the accompanying requirement of rising per-capita and per-square-kilometer values of capital-intensity and power-intensity. This desired

---

use of Riemann's work on isentropic compression as a basis for the original development of thermonuclear ignition. Such unclassified documentation was obtained, identifying this Riemann *Fortpflanzung* paper in that connection. It was at a subsequent, "report back" meeting that same year, that LaRouche underlined the application of the same paper to physical-economic modelling, and presented the set of inequalities used to create the highly successful 1980-1983 U.S. Quarterly Economic Forecast of the *Executive Intelligence Review* (**EIR**) newsweekly.

29. E.g., the brilliantly confirmed analysis provided within his *Mechanik des Ohres* (Mechanics of the Ear): **Riemann Werke**, pp. 338-350.

30. As noted, repeatedly, in other locations, this reporter has found it desirable to apportion all physical science among four functionally distinguished domains of inquiry. Two areas, astrophysics and microphysics, are domains in which the scale of phenomena is either too large, or too small, to be addressed directly by the senses. In a third area, biophysics, we deal with the principled distinction between processes, such as organic compounds, which, in one instant are functioning as part of a living process, and, in another instant, not. This also defies simple sense-perception. Those three domains, leave, as residue, the domain of macrophysics, in which sense-perception plays a larger immediate role.

result is realized, typically, by the fostering of increase of the (physical) productive powers of labor through investment in scientific and technological progress.

Consider the following summary of the relevant argument elaborated in other locations.[31]

Physical economy identifies the primary phenomena of economic processes in terms of market-baskets of both necessary physical consumption and certain crucial classes of services, limited essentially (in modern society) to education, health care, and science and technology as such. These market-baskets are defined per capita (of labor-force), per household, and per square kilometer of relevant land-area employed. The market-baskets are defined for personal consumption, for the processes of production, and for those improvements in land-area used which we class under "basic economic infrastructure." Physical economy recognizes a required functional relationship between the level of these market-baskets and the productive powers of labor, as measured in terms of both production and consumption of the content of these market-baskets.[32]

That yields an implied differential expression: What level of input (consumption) is required to maintain a certain rate of output of necessary products for consumption? Without yet knowing the exact answer to that question at any given point, the idea of the question is clear. This idea is expressed conveniently as the notion of *potential relative population-density.*[33]

The levels of combined market-basket consumption which are required to maintain not less than some constant rate of potential relative population-density, are compared to the notion of "energy of the system." Output of market-basket content in excess of those required levels, is compared to "free energy." The "free energy" is considered "not wasted," on the condition that it is consumed in market-basket forms, for both ex-panding the scale of the economy, and increasing the potential relative population-density. It the latter case, the capital-intensity ("energy of the system" per capita, per household, and per square kilometer) must increase, and the power-density must also increase. The requirement is, that the ratio of apparent "free energy" to "energy of the system" must not decrease, despite a rising relative value of "energy of the system" per capita, per household, and per square kilometer.

The increase of potential relative population-density, under the condition that those constraints are satisfied, is treated as the economic-process analog for what is expressed as "negative-entropic" evolutionary self-development of the biosphere in biology and in the terms of reference supplied by the Academician V.I. Vernadsky's notion of biogeochemistry. To avoid confusion with the "information theory's" popularized misuse of the term "negative entropy," the term "not-entropy" is employed instead.

In the field of what Academician V.I. Vernadsky defined as biogeochemistry, this requires the evolution of the biosphere, to bring the entire system to a higher state of organization; Vernadsky's argument typifies the line of thought which is otherwise encountered in various locations, including Leibniz's notion of a Universal Characteristic, and also the referenced portions of Riemann's posthumously published papers.

Wiener made a mess of everything, with the popularization of his wretched insistence that "negative entropy," for which he employed the neologism "negentropy," was no more than a reversal of the statistical entropy described by Ludwig Boltzmann's H-theorem. Contrary to Wiener's mechanistic schemes, if we account for mankind and mankind's activity as part of the planetary system, man's increased power over nature, typified by the increase of mankind's potential relative population-density,[34] is actually an increase of the relative "negative entropy," or, "not-entropy," of the planetary system as a whole. In other words, mankind's development supplies an evolutionary upward impulse to the totality of the system with which mankind interacts.

In this view of the matter, human cognition has developed within the domain of living processes, but those ecological characteristics of the human species

<hr>

31. E.g., Lyndon H. LaRouche, Jr., "Why Most Nobel Prize Economists Are Quacks," and "Non-Newtonian Mathematics for Economists." See note 6.

32. E.g., the case for household consumption was indicated by Gottfried Leibniz in **Society and Economy** (1671), which appears in English translation in **Executive Intelligence Review,** Jan. 4, 1991, pp. 12-13.

33. On "relative population-density," see Lyndon H. LaRouche, Jr., **So, You Wish to Learn All About Economics?** (New York: New Benjamin Franklin House, 1984). This introductory textbook has been published in various languages, including Russian, Ukrainian, and, most recently, Armenian.

34. per capita of labor-force, per household, and per square kilometer of relevant land-area employed.

which are entirely due to cognition, place mankind absolutely apart from and above all other living species. Thus, our universe subsumes the interaction among three distinguishable types of processes: non-living, living, and cognitive. The commonly subsuming principle governing such a universe, is Leibniz's notion of a Universal Characteristic.

For today's conventional classroom opinion, what we have just stated poses the question: "Is it not necessarily the case, that if the 'not-entropy' of society increases, that this must occur at the price of increasing the entropy of the universe with which society is interacting?" In other words, is the relationship of society to the remainder of the universe not what von Neumann's devotees term "a zero-sum game"? The crux of the issue, is that the idea of "universal entropy" is not a product of scientific discovery, but of the reckless application of an axiomatically linear, mechanistic world-view, upon the interpretation of the evidence of kinematic models of gases; on this account, there is an amusing ambiguity in the ironical meaning Norbert Wiener's work supplies to the term "gas theory."

The absurdity of the popular version of doctrines of "universal law of entropy," is suggested by the fact, that every rational effort to describe the universe in the large, is an evolutionary model, in which development is vectored as progress to relatively higher states of organization. In mathematical terms, this progress to higher states of organization is indicated by the emergence of physical systems whose characteristics can not be identified without resort to the mathematics of successively higher cardinalities. The attempt to explain the efficient directedness of such universalizing processes of emergence of higher cardinalities, renders absurd every attempt to explain the existence of matter itself in terms of a mechanistic dogma of "building blocks." The evidence is, that recognizably higher physical states of cardinality, are accomplished by transformations of the entire system, not by accretions of objects of a mechanistically fixed domain.

The counterposing of the developmental (e.g., not-entropic) and Kant-like mechanistic views is noted by Riemann, in the first of the referenced papers. Crucial is the demonstration, that, as in the case of Euler's absurd 1761 attack on Leibniz's **Monadology**, the presumption of that Kant-like, mechanistic view, from which Richard Clausius, Lord Kelvin, and Hermann Grassmann concocted

their chimerical "Second Law of Thermodynamics,"[35] is "axiomatic linearization in the small." Create a mathematics, in which all is subsumed under the axiomatic assumption, that everything in the universe is consistent with the Euclidean blind faith in the universality of perfectly continuous linear extension, even into the extremely great and the extremely small. The true believer then regards any formulation which is inconsistent with such a mathematical "proof," as "disproven," and everything which must be assumed to preserve consistency within the theorem-lattice of such a mathematics, is considered as "proven" by all of the awesomely credulous professorial, head-nodding dupes attending the relevant conference.[36]

Once we recognize, that such a mathematics constitutes no proof at all respecting the issues immediately at hand, the most generous consideration which the advocates of the "Second Law" might require of rational people, is the famous Scots' verdict, "not proven." No axiom of a mathematics is proven by the employment of the formal mathematical theorem-lattice whose existence depends upon that included assumption.

Those qualifying observations stated, situate the matter at hand. Now, turn directly to the subject of Leibniz's Universal Characteristic.

The paradigmatic form of all increase in mankind's

---

35. It was Kelvin who proposed to Clausius this radically mechanistic interpretation of Sadi Carnot's work. In this case, as in all of his attacks upon Bernhard Riemann, Clausius relied upon Hermann Grassmann for the mathematical side of his endeavors. See **Riemann Werke**, note on page 293. The crucial role which the axiomatic presumption of linearization in the small played in Grassmann's work, including all of his work on the "Second Law" and attacks upon Riemann, is reflected in his famous 1844 work founding a relevant branch of modern vector analysis, the so-called *Ausdehnungslehre*.

36. During 1978, former FEF Director Morris Levitt dug out a document authored by J. Clerk Maxwell which caused FEF much amusement at that time. In this document, Maxwell responded to the question: Why had Maxwell failed to give credit to such predecessors as Wilhelm Weber and Riemann (and also, most crucially, the founder of electrodynamics, Ampère) for many of the discoveries which Maxwell tacitly presented as either the work of Michael Faraday, or his own? To this, Maxwell replied, that "we," referring to the circles including Kelvin, et al., had chosen to disregard any work which relied upon geometries "different than our own." The same point is made, in similar terms, in Maxwell's principal work. The implication of Lord Rayleigh's denunciation of Riemann's *Fortpflanzung* paper, is the same: the root of the mechanistic world-view, which the empiricist world-outlook of modern Britain acquired from its ancient master, Paolo Sarpi, is always the presumption of the universality of percussive causality within a universe which is axiomatically linearized in the very small.

potential relative population-density, from the several millions potential of a man-like higher ape, to the billions of today, is changes in social-productive behavior typified by general application of the fruits of scientific and technological progress.[37]

Each of the transmitted discoveries is known by means of the replication of that original act of discovery within the mind of the hearer. On the condition that education of the young proceeds according to that latter principle, present-day knowledge is the accumulation of all of those singularities which valid past discoveries have conveyed to the use of the present generations: just as students today would be scientific illiterates, until they re-experience the original discoveries by the members of Plato's Academy at Athens in this way, from Plato, Eudoxus, and Theaetetus, through Eratosthenes. Without a Classical education of the young, in the great Classical works of poetry, tragedy, music, and natural science, going back to the foundations of modern civilization over 2,500 years ago, there can not be a truly civilized or even rational society, a cruel fact we see enacted so brutishly on our streets and in our government and universities today.

Each valid such discovery invokes the principle we have associated here with the topological symbol $(n+1)/n$. Each discovery is a singularity of that type. Progress in knowledge is an accumulation of such singularities. As Riemann emphasizes, within the texts provided below, that accumulation of knowledge is interactive, every new concept interacting with every other accumulated within the same mind. Thus, with every thought, this increase of singularities is reflected efficiently: in mathematical terms, the density of discontinuities for any arbitrarily selected interval of human action, is increased. It is this increase of "density of discontinuities" which typifies the form of "not-entropic" and the form of the action which generates "not-entropy" in, for example, the form of increase of society's potential relative population-density.

The crucial fact is, that this increase of knowledge, as defined in this way, is consistently efficient. *The universe obeys the human creative-mental powers' command!* Thus, as **Genesis 1** prescribes, mankind exerts dominion over nature. Conversely, the universe is manifestly so constituted, that it is prone to submit to the authority of that power of creative reason which is a potentiality peculiar to the individual human personality.

By accumulating a reliving of the original valid acts of discovery of principle, which constitute the accumulation of human knowledge to the present date, we are enabled to recognize the distinguishing features of that form of act of creative reason, by means of which valid discoveries have been commonly achieved. That experience becomes known to us, as to Johannes Kepler, as *Reason*, or, as for Gottfried Leibniz, as *necessary and sufficient reason*. Once we recognize, that mankind's cumulative development of knowledge represents the power of the human will to command the universe according to the law embedded in that universe, we have shown ourselves that *reason* as we define it *subjectively* in this way, is also an efficient approximation of Reason as it exists, ostensibly *objectively*, as an efficient principle pervading the universe as a whole.

What we recognize in the form of "not-entropy," as in the increase of society's potential relative population-density, is the characteristic of Reason, both as it exists efficiently, "objectively" within the universe at large, and as we are able to adduce the principles of reason, "subjectively," through the efficiency of valid discoveries of principle in the domains of science and art.

Once that is acknowledged, then it is clear to us, that the universe is not linearized in the extremely small, or extremely large. It is "not-entropic," in the extremely small and extremely large, alike. To see this more clearly, it was sufficient, to shift the emphasis in reading Riemann's contributions to mathematical physics, away from physics narrowly conceived, back to the vantage-point of Leibniz, the vantage-point of physical economy, the vantage-point of the efficient relationship between valid human individual reason, and man's increased power over the universe. Thus, we may say, that not-entropy, as reflected in type by Riemann's topological expression $(n+1)/n$, corresponds to what Leibniz named a Universal Characteristic.

____

37. This progress in the human condition is not due only to scientific and technological progress. The metaphors which arise from Classical forms of poetry, tragedy, and music have as crucial a role in increasing man's power to exist as what we term conventionally "natural science." Nonetheless, as we have already indicated, valid fundamental scientific discoveries merely typify the more general case for all forms of expression of the creative-mental powers of persons as metaphor: as the great English poet Percy Shelley expressed the point, within his "A Defence of Poetry": the "power of communicating and receiving intense and impassioned conceptions respecting man and nature." What is stated above, here, should be read with the understanding that the case for scientific ideas *typifies* the case for metaphor in general.

www.ingramcontent.com/pod-product-compliance
Lightning Source LLC
Chambersburg PA
CBHW081602270726
48657CB00029B/3471

9781729595992